Tim Wright

BRITISH CELTIC COINS
ART OR IMITATION?

An introduction to the coins of pre-Roman Britain

FOUNDED 1666
SPINK
WHERE HISTORY IS VALUED

First published in 2023 by Spink and Son Ltd

A CIP catalogue record for this book is available from the British Library.

ISBN 978-1-912667-98-7

Typeset by Russell Whittle, Litmus Graphics

Printed and bound by Gutenberg Press, Malta

Spink and Son Ltd

69 Southampton Row

London WC1B 4ET

www.spinkbooks.com

ACKNOWLEDGEMENTS

This book is intended as an introduction to the coins of pre-Roman Britain, through my own experience of collection and study. In the absence of contemporary accounts by the peoples who produced them, we are left with the coins themselves and circumstantial evidence to interpret them. The inevitable result is conjecture and controversy. What follows is a selection of coins and a personal perspective. Neither the coins nor the commentary can claim to be exhaustive. Rather, they are intended as a 'teaser' to stimulate interest in the subject.

Like many, I started collecting ancient Greek coins, but diversified into Roman Republican, and then settled on pre-Roman British 'Celtic' coins as my primary focus. Dominic Chorney, at A H Baldwin in London, and Shanna Schmidt, who runs her own business and partners with NAC (Numismatica Ars Classica) in the US, both guided and facilitated my early collecting. Elizabeth Cottam, at Chris Rudd coins, introduced me to the community of ancient British coins and has been the source of most of the coins illustrated in this book.

The book started its life as a catalogue of my own collection, prefaced by some explanations, which I shared with Chris Rudd. He encouraged me to drop the catalogue and expand the introduction, around the theme of 'crude copies or inspired originals'. This led to further reading and research, aided by input from John Talbot, who felt there was a place for a more accessible introduction to the subject.

Courtney Nimura, curator at the Ashmolean Museum who also oversees the CCID (Celtic Coin Index Digital) at the School of Archaeology in Oxford, generously guided me from a rough draft to a publishable book, aided by input from Philip de Jersey and Daphne Nash Briggs. Thus, I have been fortunate in having various drafts and parts of this book read by some of the leading figures in the field, although I take sole responsibility for its opinions, errors and omissions.

This book is deliberately visual and includes images of over a hundred coins, all from my photographs but aided by Adele Armistead's skilful formatting. I am grateful to Emma Howard and her colleagues at Spink for supporting this project and helping me navigate the process of finalising the manuscript and publishing the book. Finally, I would like to thank my family for indulging my distraction with this project.

Tim Wright
La Maioun, France. June 2023

CONTENTS

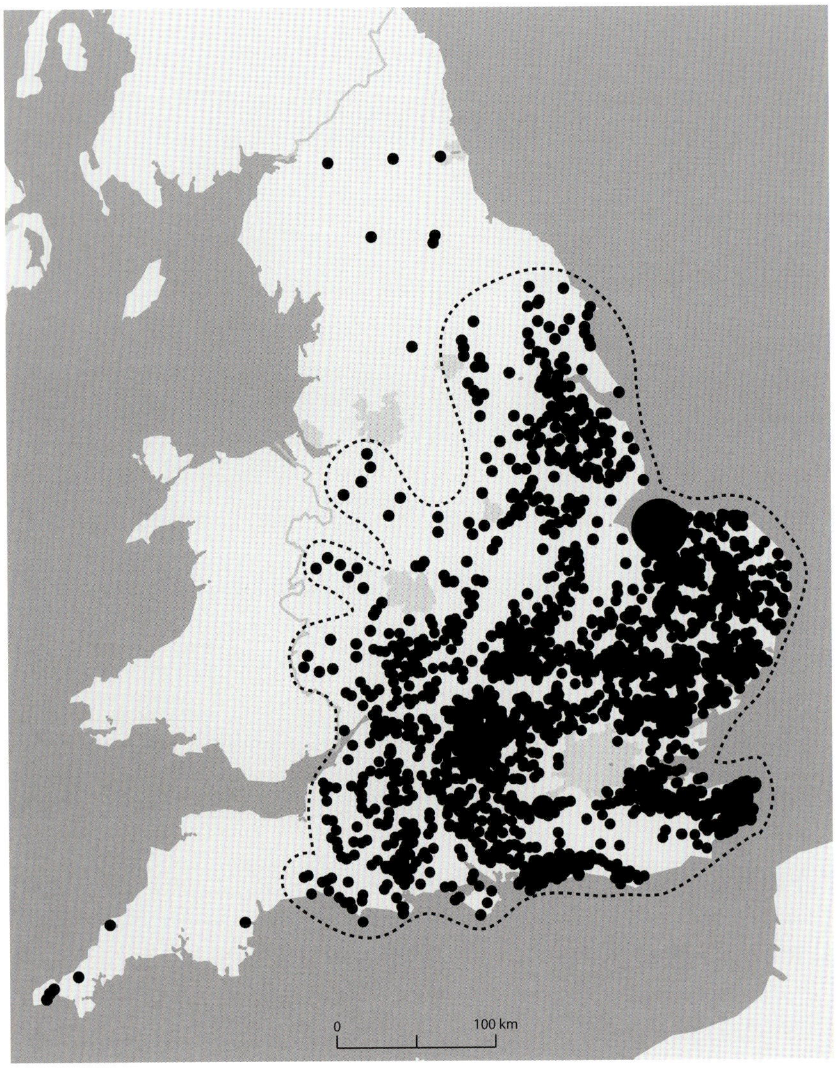

Fig. 1.1. Most coins have been found in England, south of the Humber and east of Wales and Devon

Source: Celtic Coin Index
(basemap: Esri UK, Esri, HERE, Garmin, FAO, NOAA, USGS)

1.

CONTEXT AND CONTROVERSY

Over two thousand years ago, some of the inhabitants of what we now call England started to produce coins and continued to do so for over a century until the Roman conquest. Who these peoples were, why they adopted coinage, and the origin of their designs have long been debated. What is less controversial is the extraordinary variety and complexity of these coins, which make them worthy of collection and study.

Our starting point is with the coins themselves and where they were found. Over one hundred thousand coins have been discovered by professionals and amateurs alike, with a growing number in recent years associated with the explosion of metal detecting. Most finds are south of the Humber and east of Wales and Devon, suggesting that the primary coin producers and users of the time were in these areas (Fig. 1.1). Their context and composition allow us to date most coins to between the early-first century BCE, before Caesar's invasion, and the middle of the first century CE after the Claudian conquest (see Appx 3).

The coins come in a variety of metals and sizes. Like Olympic medals, they are gold, silver or bronze. Denominations include staters, quarter staters, units, half units and minims (see Appx 1). At 7–24 mm in diameter and 0.3–7.3 g in weight, they are lightweights compared with other coins of the ancient and modern worlds. Although only marginally smaller, the gold stater is two-thirds of the weight of its Macedonian equivalent or the modern British sovereign. The most common silver unit is a quarter of the weight of a Greek *drachm* or Roman *denarius* and a sixth of the weight of a Euro, British pound or US dollar. The smallest coin, the silver minim, is less than half the weight of the smallest Greek coin, the *obol* and a sixth of a US or Euro cent and a tenth of a British penny.

The composition of the coins also tells a story of scarcity and craftsmanship. Just looking at the gold of a stater or quarter stater tells you that it is different from other ancient and modern coins. They are frequently 'redder' or 'whiter', due to higher copper and silver content respectively, with gold sometimes comprising less than half the metal (compared with 92% for a modern sovereign). Equally, the bronze coins, made from copper and tin (in a ratio of *c.* 6:1) may also have traces of lead and iron, as 'potins', which turns them from an initially silvery to an almost black colour over time.

Occasionally, the dies or casts for making coins are also found, or their use may be discerned from the coins themselves. This provides a strong indication of how the coins were made. Hammered coins (the majority) were made by producing a blank 'flan', probably heated, which was then struck between two dies made of a harder metal, such as a high tin content bronze, judging from the few surviving examples. The dies were not flat, but rather dished, with the obverse side being more convex and the reverse side being more concave. Alternatively, a clay mould may be used, where the design is either inscribed into the clay or impressed through a wooden model made of wood, into which the molten metal was poured, and then the coins produced by cutting the runlets that connect them.

Coin types may be distinguished according to their denomination and the imagery created by the dies. Dies wear out over time, so by identifying the specific dies used for a particular coin, it is possible to sequence coin types into a relative chronology. Where possible, this process is aided by the location and context of the find, as well as the other coins found. In this way, at least a thousand distinct coin types have been identified, with frequent new variations and even types discovered from new finds.

The coins themselves go some way to telling us how, where and when they were produced. Yet, even where they are inscribed, they do not resolve the fierce debate about who produced these coins. This identity crisis takes three forms: the peoples, their 'tribes' and their 'leaders'. The peoples of pre-Roman Britain have variously been described as Ancient Britons, Late Iron Age Britons, or Celtic Britons (or British Celts). None is entirely satisfactory, but the last is probably most prevalent, and yet still questionable.

The word 'Celt' comes from the Greek *keltoi* and was used by Herodotus to describe the peoples of the Danube and possibly Iberia, rather than Britain. The Romans corrupted another Greek word, *pritani* (meaning 'painted ones'), to describe the inhabitants as *Brittanni*. It was not until the eighteenth century that 'Celtic' was adopted to describe the peoples of Ireland, Scotland, and Wales. Following the archaeological discoveries at Hallstatt and La Tène in the nineteenth century, the term was adopted to describe the peoples of much of continental Europe and most of Britain, who were deemed to be part of a shared 'civilisation'. More recently the notion of a Celtic Britain, let alone a Celtic Europe, has been challenged, with even the very existence of Celts questioned. The word 'Celt' has generally been dropped in favour of a much looser grouping of more diverse 'Celtic peoples' across much of Europe, who shared some aspects of the same culture and were at least partially connected (see Appendices 2 and 3 for a chronology).

In Britain, the debate has coincided with the dismantling of the Union and has therefore become politicised. Whether all of Britain or just its northern and western periphery are described as 'Celtic' continues to be debated. If the latter, then the very regions that produced coins, the south and east, should not be described as Celtic. As the evidence remains equivocal, this book has decided to retain the simplest descriptor of *British Celtic Coins* but acknowledges the controversy with the addition of the more accurate *Coins of pre-Roman Britain*. For the remainder of the book, I will use the broadly understood label 'Celtic coins', but without the supporting notion that they were made by a specific group called 'the Celts'.

The second part of the 'identity' crisis relates to the adoption of 'tribes' and the attribution of coins to them. With at least a thousand types, there is enormous variation in the design of coins from this period. These variations have been mapped to particular types according to style, find location and, where present, inscription. Yet there has been an increasing tendency to attribute almost all coins not only to a broad geographic region but to tribal groupings derived from the *civitas*, or administrative districts, adopted by the Romans after conquest. While some of these tribes were mentioned by Caesar in the mid-first century BCE, the comprehensive mapping of Britain's 'tribes' is found in the work of the second century CE geographer, Ptolemy. Even though this was more than a century after-the-fact (of coin production), it has been increasingly adopted as a numismatic typology.

This practice started with inscribed coins being assigned to a hybrid of regional and tribal groups by Evans in the nineteenth century. From the mid-twentieth century, even uninscribed coins were distributed across tribal groups, first by Mack and then by Van Arsdell and others. In the last thirty years, there has been an explosion in discoveries of new uninscribed coin types, in particular, all of which are linked to specific tribes in the standard reference work, *Ancient British Coins* ('ABC'), published in 2010.

Ian Leins has challenged the adoption of Roman *civitas* as pre-Roman coin-producing tribes. He contends that it is unlikely that all or even most of these administrative districts reflected the socio-political organisation prior to conquest. Rather these groupings were likely more fluid comprising different sub-groups, together with shifting boundaries over time. A geographic rather than 'tribal' model is probably more reliable in mapping coins according to recognisable stylistic differences. Thus, the thirteen coin-producing 'tribes' are grouped into seven regions: the South-Western (*Durotriges*), Western (*Dobunni* and *East Wiltshire*), Southern (*Atrebates*, *Belgae*, *Berkshire*, *Regini* and *Vectuarii*), Kent (*Cantiaci*), North Thames (*Catuvellauni* and *Trinovantes*), East Anglian (*Iceni*) and North-Eastern (*Corieltavi*), broadly following those used in ABC (Appx 4).

The third and final part of the identity crisis relates to tribal 'leaders', as expressed on the inscriptions of the coins. The assumption is that the inscription refers to a chieftain or even king of a particular tribe and that they were the issuing authority for the coins. In this way, multiple 'leaders' have been 'discovered' from inscriptions, assigned to a particular tribe and sequenced in time and through a given lineage.

This approach is not without merit, at least for the known 'dynasties' of the south-east, being the descendants of Commios in the Southern region, and the family of Cunobelinus in the North Thames region. Some of the characters are referenced in historic sources and corroborated through inscriptions (see Appx 5). Yet, such an approach has also been applied to the other coin-producing regions, where there is little further evidence in support of either the individuals or indeed the leadership models that have been imputed. More likely there were a variety of social hierarchies, some elected, others hereditary, with different powers vested in those referenced.

It should also be acknowledged that the inscriptions, outside the south-east, may reference moneyers rather than leaders, or mint locations rather than individuals. Equally, similarities of style and imagery on coins should not of themselves imply that they were produced by the same 'tribal leader' but may have reflected wandering expert engravers. Suffice to say that a degree of caution should be adopted when ascribing a particular coin to either a tribe or particular leader, unless there is other evidence to support this. It is the mystery and controversy that makes these coins so interesting and fun.

The next source of controversy relates to the adoption of coinage in Britain. When did coinage come to Britain? How was the practice transmitted? And what were coins used for? These debates have raged from the nineteenth century to the present day and involved some of the leading lights on ancient British numismatics. While the questions are clearly related, for example transmission by trade also talks to use, I will cover each of these in turn.

The overall chronology for coinage in Britain is relatively uncontroversial. Imported coins, dated to the first half of the second century BCE, circulated in parts of Britain during the late second and early first centuries BCE. This was followed by local production, which started shortly before or about the time of Caesar's invasion, in the middle of the first century BCE and lasted until shortly after the Roman conquest in the middle of the first century CE. Coins continued to circulate after the Romans arrived, but both production and usage was then displaced with Roman issues in the second half of the first century CE.

Our confidence in this overall chronology comes from coin finds in Britain and the Continent, especially hoards, which provide helpful context to an individual coin. To massively oversimplify, the latest known coin in a hoard provides a rough guide to the earliest point at which it could have been buried. The presence of different denominations in the same hoard (for example, Roman and Celtic) provides some indication of circulation. Yet production is more difficult to pin down than usage, as there is evidence that some issues were used long after their manufacture. Moreover, by comparing finds on the Continent and Britain, we can make an informed judgement about whether coins were imported or locally produced.

The chronological debate has centred on when native production of coins started. The spectacular 'large' or 'broad flan' gold stater [Fig. 1.2] was correctly dated by nineteenth century numismatists to the first half of the second century BCE. The debate centred on whether it was a local or imported coin; in other words, whether it was produced in Britain or the neighbouring continent. It involved two gentlemen named John: Akerman and Evans. Akerman argued, correctly as it turned out, that it was an import and that native production only started around the time of Caesar's invasion. Evans, who we will hear about later, 'won' the argument, by asserting, incorrectly, that this was the first British production.

The next 'adoption' debate centred on how the practice of using and producing coins was transmitted to Britain, and indeed other regions before that. There are multiple theories, based on invasion, mercenaries and trade. These have gone in and out of fashion with time and are closely related to the question of what coins were used for. For the present, we will focus on transmission.

Writing in the 1950s, the retired naval officer and avid collector Commander RP Mack attributed the adoption of coinage in Britain to two major 'Belgic' invasions. After correctly classifying the early finds as continental imports he proceeded to describe a first invasion in around 75 BCE, centred on the Thames, resulting in settlement in Kent and the adoption of the 'invaders' coinage. The second Belgic invasion followed Caesar's (invading Britain was clearly popular at the time!), and this time centred on the Solent, and resulted in settlement in southern Britain, where coinage was adopted and local production was started.

The appeal of invasion theories is that they provide a neat solution to rapid changes in society, in this case the adoption of coinage.

Fig. 1.2. One of the earliest and most beautiful coins found in Britain was imported from the Continent

Gallo-Belgic, *Bellovaci, c.* 150–125 BCE,
'Broad Flan' uninscribed gold stater (ABC 4) – Scale 1:2.3

Roman writers, such as Tacitus and Caesar, explained similarities between the coastal peoples of Britain and those of Gaul (modern day France and Belgium) as resulting from invasion and settlement. Such views persisted into the twentieth century but are now generally discounted through lack of archaeological evidence of a uniformly violent transition.

Writing thirty-four years later, the academic Daphne Nash Briggs maintained some aspects of Mack's invasion thesis with respect to Britain but focused much more on the role of mercenaries as a transmission mechanism, particularly during its early period of adoption in the Danube region during the fourth and third centuries BCE. Celtic mercenaries were employed by Greeks, Carthaginians, and Macedonians who upon returning to their communities adopted the practice and designs of the gold and silver coins they had received. Nash observes that Rome's rise to dominance effectively curtailed this activity, preferring to use auxillaries. As such, mercenary activity became localised with one community employing the warriors of another, and controlling coinage to do so. Twenty years later, Philip de Jersey confirmed that mercenary activity was generally seen as the primary transmission mechanism. We will also see that the payment of mercenaries was one of the major uses of coins.

Trade is similarly both a means of transmitting the practice of coinage and a major use. For us, it is a much more intuitive explanation and corresponds to modern uses of money. It was a favoured explanation in the nineteenth century not least by Evans, who saw it as the primary means by which coins were imported in exchange for goods like slaves and possibly mercenaries. A century later, academics like Derek Allen rejected it in favour of other theories, given that barter was viewed as the dominant mechanism for exchange. In recent years, it has been revived by John Talbot, at least with respect to the coinage of Britain's so-called *Iceni* tribe, of what is now Norfolk.

We have already touched on the role of coins in paying for mercenaries or as an exchange mechanism for trade, but these are not alone as in describing the function of coins. In recent years, more political or cultural explanations have been adopted. For academics like John Creighton and John Sills, the function of coins was primarily political, associated with the payment of tribute (most notably, to Caesar, following his invasion) or the distribution of patronage, and was therefore concentrated among the political elite and leadership.

By looking at the context of major finds, including archaeological sites, a potentially different interpretation has been developed. Britain's largest coin find of the period is the 'Hallaton Treasure', found in 2000 in south-east Leicestershire. In one go, the find doubled the number of North-Eastern *Corieltavi* coins known, to ten thousand. This well-preserved site suggests that coins were used for votive offerings, over a prolonged period. Leins believes that the site was associated with ritual sacrifice and/or feasting.

Leins describes a more nuanced archaeological approach to understanding the relationship between material culture (including coins) and society, which presents a hybrid interpretation to the adoption of coins and their function. While migration (rather than invasion) and mercenary activity may have been an initial catalyst for the need for coins, their usage was likely sustained by patronage, trade and even religious practices.

So, what was the primary role of coins? If coins were only used by a sub-set of society, then it is likely that their use was associated with activities that this elite controlled, be it patronage, payment of mercenaries, religious offerings or trade. The latter, either within Britain or more likely cross-border, appears to be the most compelling.

The debate that informs the central theme of this book relates to the artistic merit of pre-Roman British coins. As we will see in the next chapter, it is possible to trace the origins of these coins with those of the adjacent Continent and all the way back to Macedonian prototypes and beyond. In the last chapter, we will also explore the adoption of Roman imagery and even specific coin designs. With such 'bookends' of external influences, there is a debate about whether pre-Roman British coins were 'crude replicas' or 'innovative originals'. Put another way, were they *Art* or *Imitation*?

Even using the word 'art' in this context is highly controversial. There is a long-standing debate about whether prehistoric material culture, such as coins, should be described as art at all. By 'prehistoric' we mean a period before written accounts, which could provide what Courtney Nimura describes as an 'insider story' that explains what the artist might have been thinking. The stories that survive from this period are by Roman outsiders, which are far from reliable. Taking coins out of their context and seeking to evaluate their artistic merit is clearly fraught with danger, not least more than two thousand years later. Yet, as Richard Bradley concludes, in the absence of alternatives, we should ask the reader to assume that the term is perpetually in inverted commas.

The American numismatist RD Van Arsdell makes a distinction between 'art' and 'craft'. In his view, craftsmanship is the often highly skilled replication of an existing object, in this case a copy of a coin. Artistry, by contrast, is the creation of something original. Of course, we know that this appears on a spectrum of grey rather than black and white given the influence of early work on subsequent innovation. This book uses the term 'art' in this narrow sense, to convey originality and creativity of design rather than imply notions of aesthetics.

In the world of ancient numismatics, 'Celtic' coins, including those from Britain, are traditionally seen as poor relations or stepchildren in comparison with Greek or Roman 'classics'. In most auctions, they are merely a preamble to the 'Greeks'. This may be a function of more limited supply and demand, but it is also reflective of a broader prejudice. Roman commentators had an interest in portraying Britain as a wild and dangerous place on the edge of the world, populated (like the rest of the non-Roman world) by dangerous, uncivilised 'barbarians'. No doubt this justified a civilising invasion and conquest by the Romans and added to the glory of the conquerors. The other historical prejudice comes from the pioneer of pre-Roman British numismatics, Sir John Evans. He traced British coins back to a Macedonian prototype. Rather than discern a positive evolution he saw a 'degradation', whereby the beauty of the classical original was progressively simplified and diminished.

When these two prejudices are combined with the early influence of Gallo-Belgic prototypes and later adoption of Roman imagery, what emerges is the view that pre-Roman British coins are somehow inferior. Part of the mission of this book is to correct this damaging stereotype, by sharing the images of the coins themselves.

The theme of *Art or Imitation* is explored through the following seven chapters. Appropriately, we start with the Origins, exploring some Gallo-Belgic, Macedonian, Greek and Roman prototypes, with a view to understanding how their format, subject or designs were incorporated into pre-Roman British coins. The next three chapters explore the variety and creativity of early coins: starting with the Heads (mostly deities), flipping to the Tails (i.e. horses) and then looking at other Beasts (boars, dragons, snakes, etc). This is followed by two chapters on the specifically British developments of hidden faces and inscriptions on coins; the former likely conveying a message from the engraver and the latter probably being part of a concerted campaign of self-promotion by their 'clients'. We end with the theme of 'romanisation', particularly in the first century CE, exploring how Roman images and even specific coin designs were adopted on pre-Roman British coins, even if local identity was retained.

As if we had not encountered enough controversy, the term I have used in the final chapter is itself one of the most controversial. 'Romanisation' is used to describe the progressive adoption of Roman culture by its provinces. This obviously has relevance to the adoption of Roman imagery on British coins in the half century before conquest. Yet, in our post-colonial or indeed anti-colonial world, even the suggestion of a 'civilising' justification for conquest is clearly problematic. And, for this reason, the term has largely been discarded. Its use here is not intended to re-open that debate but rather to describe, more narrowly, the adoption of Roman imagery in the period preceding conquest.

I have not taken a firm position on most of the controversies summarised previously but have adopted some conventions that are worth highlighting. I have used both 'British Celtic coins' and 'Coins of pre-Roman Britain' interchangeably, even if the word 'Celtic' remains disputed despite common usage, and 'pre-Roman' is not entirely correct, given continued coin use following Roman conquest.

I have adopted regional rather than 'tribal' descriptions for coin types (see Appx 4), although I have kept the *civitas* in the full reference. Inscriptions are included in describing the coins, but I have only assumed that they relate to leaders where these are referenced in another source (see Appx 5). Finally, I have adopted ABC (*Ancient British Coins*) references where available, but not the names as they are not universally accepted. I hope that these conventions achieve the right balance between acknowledging debates whilst making the book easy to navigate.

In the interests of flow, there are no detailed references in the narrative. The aim is to provide an overview of the subject through a selection of coins under each theme. For those readers who are interested in going into more detail, an extensive bibliography is provided at the end. There are also a series of Appendices, with an overall explanation of terms (Appx 1), providing further context through a chronology (Appendices 2 and 3), and mapping of 'tribes' and 'authorities' to regions (Appendices 4 and 5). Each chapter includes images of some of the coins discussed. This visualisation is important and has been neglected in some of the literature on the subject. I have drawn on coins from my own collection throughout, in order to provide a collector's perspective. If the goal is to demonstrate the artistry of British Celtic coins, what better way of doing so than letting the coins speak for themselves?

2.

ORIGINS – CURSE OF PROTOTYPES

Britain was the last place in present-day Europe to adopt Celtic coins but also the place where they were produced for longer than any other. This makes it a particularly interesting region in which to examine the early influences on Celtic coins, as well as their subsequent development.

The nineteenth century polymath-cum-businessman, Sir John Evans, traced British Celtic coins back through a 'family-tree' of Gallo-Belgic types to their original *prototype* in the form of the gold stater of Philip II of Macedon, known as the 'Philippus' (Fig. 2.1). Breakthroughs in geology led Evans, like his contemporary Charles Darwin, to adopt an evolutionary approach. Yet, unlike Darwin, he mapped a deterioration in coins rather than the improvement in species. He saw the prototype simplified and degraded over time. Attitudes have changed, with a growing appreciation for so-called Celtic Art. Derek Allen for example, observed a process of disintegration, abstraction and reintegration, through which something original, innovative and artistic was created.

It is easy to see why Evans was so enamoured by the 'Philippus'. It is an exceptionally elegant coin, in the best classical Greek tradition of exquisite naturalistic realism. The obverse shows the head of Apollo, wearing a laurel wreath. The reverse shows a wonderfully executed

Fig. 2.1. Sir John Evans traced British Celtic coins back to the 'Philippus'

Kings of Macedon, Philip II or Alexander III, Pella, *c.* 340/36–328 BCE, gold stater – Scale 1:2.9

charioteer, holding a *kentron* (a sharp stick or whip) in one hand and reins in the other, driving a *biga* (two-horsed chariot). This beautifully engraved coin was almost certainly not an entirely original work of art. According to Colin Kraay, the subject and possibly prototype for Apollo was to be found on the coins of the Chalkidian League, who Philip II had just conquered, together with their gold mines. The reverse resembles some of the racing chariot imagery from the Greek city states of Sicily (Fig. 4.1) and possibly references the victory of Philip II's horse at the Olympic Games of 356 BCE. The point is that even *the* prototype celebrated by Evans was far from being entirely original, although nobody would doubt the fine artistry of its engraver.

It would also be wrong to think in terms of a single 'golden source'. In his later work, Evans recognised more than one prototype and admitted that the process of imitation was not entirely linear. Ninety years later, Allen went much further to describe a comprehensive model whereby Europe was divided into three principal material zones. The first was a bronze-producing region in north-east Spain. The second was a silver belt, from the Atlantic coast south of the Loire to the mouth of the Danube. And, the third was a golden belt, comprising northern France, Belgium and Britain, as well as south-western Germany, Switzerland, Czechoslovakia and Bohemia.

Other Macedonian types saw widespread adoption. Philip II's silver *tetradrachm* was used and then adopted as a prototype in the Danube region. The *tetradrachm* of his son, Alexander III, The Great (Fig. 2.2), was produced in vast numbers to pay mercenaries, which as we have seen was an important catalyst for transmission. Trade was a more likely stimulus for adoption of prototypes from Greek city states, such as the *nomos* of Tarus (present day Tarentum) cited by Evans and the *drachm* of Massalia (Marseille) highlighted by Allen (both in Fig. 2.2). The considerable influence of Roman coins and imagery on British Celtic coins will be explored in Chapter Eight, yet Roman coins were themselves also heavily influenced by those of the Greek and Macedonian world.

Fig. 2.2. There were multiple classical prototypes for continental Celtic coins

(Top–bottom)
Kings of Macedon, Pella, Philip II, *c.* 336/5–329/8 BCE, silver *tetradrachm* – Scale 1:1.6; Kings of Macedon, Alexander III, Amphipolis, *c.* 323–320 BCE, silver *tetradrachm* – Scale 1:1.4; Gaul, Massalia, *c.* 125–90 BCE, *silver drachm* – Scale 1:2.3

The Republic was a relatively late adopter of coinage, only doing so around the time of the Pyrrhic War of *c.* 280–275 BCE. With no tradition of coinage, they probably outsourced early *didrachms* to Greek city states of southern Italy. The first coins were an unsurprising hybrid (Fig. 2.3). The style and format ('heads and tails') was very Greek and even included Carthaginian elements (Siculo-Punic; see, for example, Fig. 4.1). But the subject (Mars) and branding ('ROMA') were clearly Roman. The *denarius* was introduced at the end of the third century BCE and became the default Roman silver coin for over four centuries. Early issues maintained the format, with the patron goddess, Roma, on the obverse and familiar chariots or *Dioscuri* horsemen on the reverse. Although later Roman coins adopted other imagery that reflected the family or political agenda of the moneyer of the time, the early issues exhibited considerable Greek and Macedonian influences.

Returning to the Philippus prototype, we see that the classical image was gradually transformed into a more abstract design, capturing the essence of the original and incorporating local elements. This process may either be viewed as one of crude imitation or artistic innovation. We know that Evans was distressed at the almost sacrilegious simplification and distortion of the complex and artistic original. While Allen agreed that the early Celtic coins were little more than forgeries, he saw them subsequently transformed through true artistic innovations. Today, there is much greater appreciation of the 'art' of pre-Roman Iron Age peoples, including that expressed on their coins. It requires us to suspend our preconceptions about art, to engage with their ambiguous and dream-like quality, where there are only suggestions of representation and the results are highly stylised or abstract.

We see this process on the reverse of the Macedonian prototype, whereby the *biga* is gradually replaced by a semi-naturalistic charioteer and a single horse, and then finally a single horse, disjointed and abstracted with pellets and crescents forming the horse's outline and the remnants of the charioteer (e.g. Fig. 2.4). On the obverse of the Philippus, we see a process

Fig. 2.3. Roman coins were also modelled on Greek prototypes

(Top–bottom)
Roman Republic, Anon. Issue, Romano-Campanian, *c.* 240 BCE, silver *didrachm* – Scale 1:1.9; Roman Republic, L. Saufeius, Rome, *c.* 152 BCE, silver *denarius* – Scale 1:2.2; Roman Republic, C. Terentius Lucanus, Rome, *c.* 147 BCE, silver *denarius* – Scale 1:2.2

whereby the face of Apollo is gradually diminished and then replaced with an abstract wreathed head and becomes the prototype for British coins (Fig. 3.2). It would be wrong to see this as a linear process but rather one with numerous local developments, variations and innovations.

A wonderful, if very common, example is the silver stater of the Coriosolites (Fig. 2.5). While we cannot be certain, it is possible that the obverse shows Ogmios, the local equivalent to the sun-god Apollo. Major Norman Rybot, who studied the coins of the Coriosolites intensively in the nineteen-thirties, characterised their designs as eccentric, verging on madness, yet without question clever and well-executed art.

Closer to Britain were the Morini, the 'sea people' of what is now the Pas-de-Calais. They did not follow the Philippus prototype but instead developed their own distinctive brand of coinage, which was also replicated and adopted by the so-called *Durotriges* of South-Western Britain, presumably due to close trading ties (see Fig. 2.5).

The curse of prototypes, whether Macedonian or Gallo-Belgic, is that they imply that British Celtic coins were unoriginal copies rather than artistic originals. Yet this logic is flawed in two key respects: there is very little that is truly original without any prior influences, and even if there is, it does not preclude the possibility of 'artistic' creativity. We have seen that there was not one but multiple prototypes, including Macedonian, Greek and Roman. Many, if not most, of these were in turn influenced by other coins, not least the Macedonian and Roman coins by the earlier Greeks. While it is possible to map multiple lineages for many coins, this is not a linear process, and instead there are lots of twists and turns. Frequently the influence of the prototype is form over substance, as demonstrated by the enduring adoption of the 'heads and tails' model retained to this day (e.g. Fig. 2.6).

We have also seen that the development from a prototype is not necessarily an artistic downward spiral but that it is more evolution

Fig. 2.4. Gaulish coins adopted the Macedonian prototype but then reduced it to its core elements and added their own twists

Reverse of Gaul, *Eburovices, c.* 75–50 BCE, gold half stater (Scheers Class 3: LT 7019 var.) – Scale 1:2.9; reverse of Gaul, *Ambiani, c.* 50 BCE, gold stater (ABC 16) – Scale 1:3.2

Fig. 2.6. The 'heads and tails' format of Greek, Macedonian, Roman and Gaulish prototypes was adopted in pre-Roman Britain, and has been remarkably enduring for over two thousand years

Britain, Elizabeth II, 2013, gold sovereign – Scale 1:2.5

than degradation. It may start with imitation but then it proceeds through a plethora of innovations, be they abstract, stylised, surreal or just plain magical. It would be absurd to say that one is 'better' than the other but rather they are successively different and creative. Having hopefully gone some way towards lifting the curse of the prototype, we will now start to explore pre-Roman British coins themselves, and how they uniquely blend external influences with local innovations.

3.

HEADS – MAGICAL SURREALISM

'Heads' are almost ubiquitous on the obverse of coins from antiquity to the present day. In the case of pre-Roman British coins, heads feature frequently, but not universally; in some cases, the head is clearly discernible, while in others it has been abstracted to an unrecognisable motif.

We saw in the previous chapter that Gaulish coins generally adopted the Philippus prototype, with the head of Apollo, in profile, on its obverse. This image was abstracted into a wreathed motif and then reinvented through a range of local subjects and styles. British Celtic coins followed suit, adopting the Gallo-Belgic prototype for gold coins and evolving the designs to become intricate wreath motifs. Silver coinage was less conservative and saw an explosion of innovation, including a wonderful range of heads, as well as animal images (Chapter 5). In the later period, the obverse of gold and silver coins started to be inscribed with the names and emblems of tribal leaders, replacing heads as the dominant image (see Chapter 7). Yet, if we look at British Celtic coins in aggregate, heads are present on a significant proportion.

In the classical world heads were a common feature on the obverse of coins, invariably depicting gods then transitioning to leaders, with some

Fig. 3.1. Heads were very common on Greek coins, usually depicting a deity, such as Apollo, Athena, Arethusa, Persephone, Tanit or Melkart

(Clockwise from top-right)
Reverse of Sicily, Leontini, *c.* 450–440 BCE, silver *tetradrachm* – Scale 1:1.5; obverse of Attica, Athens, *c.* 510–490 BCE, silver *drachm* – Scale 1:2.3; reverse of Sicily, Syracuse, *c.* 405–400 BCE, silver *decadrachm* – Scale 1:1.1; obverse of Lokris, Lokri Opuntii, *c.* 340 BCE, silver *stater* – Scale 1:1.6; obverse of North Africa, Carthage, *c.* 300–260 BCE, silver *shekel* – Scale 1:1.9; obverse of Carthage, Second Punic War, *c.* 220–205 BCE, silver half *shekel* – Scale 1:1.7

hybrids along the way. The coins of Greek city states typically reference their patron gods, frequently associated with their foundation myth (see Fig. 3.1 for a selection). For example Syracuse adopted the goddess Arethusa, who in mythology fled her home in Arcadia by swimming under the sea and resurfacing in the fountains of Syracuse. As we saw in the last chapter, Philip II of Macedon adopted the patron god of the Chalkidian League, Apollo (Fig. 2.1), following their conquest. When Alexander III ('The Great') succeeded his father to the throne, the Apollo image was retained for gold *staters* but, like the silver *tetradrachm* portraying Herakles (Fig. 2.2), started to blend Alexander's own features with those of the god. Rome went through a similar transition. Once the Republic had embraced coinage, the image of its patron God, Roma, became a dominant obverse theme (see Fig. 2.3). As the Republic ended, we see the emergence of oligarchs, dictators and ultimately Emperors emerging as the portrait on Roman coins.

The heads portrayed on British Celtic coins went through a different evolution. They adopted a Gallo-Belgic prototype that had already replaced the face of Apollo with an abstract representation of a wreathed head. This then went through a process of further abstraction to produce an image that bore little or no resemblance to the original portrait of the god (Fig. 3.2). These images beg some important questions. Are we still looking at the face of Apollo or have we transitioned to decorative art? If the former, is it merely a crude simplification of the original or has it created something new and distinctive? And, with respect to British coins, are they just copies of the Gallo-Belgic prototypes or has the process of abstraction extended the artistic process?

As we saw in the previous chapter, the answers to these questions were very different in the nineteenth to the twentieth century. Such designs received much greater appreciation in the context of developments in modern art. For example, the surrealist André Breton was an avid collector of Gaulish coins. Although as we saw in the first chapter, calling prehistoric material culture 'art' is controversial and attempts to equate it

Fig. 3.2. The default head for many gold (and some silver) pre-Roman British coins is the abstracted Apollo, based on Gallo-Belgic prototypes

Obverse of North-Eastern, *Corieltavi, c.* 60–50 BCE, uninscribed gold stater (ABC 1719) – Scale 1:2.9; obverse of South-Western, *Durotriges, c.* 58–45 BCE, uninscribed silver stater (ABC 2163) – Scale 1:3.2

to modern art are largely discredited, like the 1984 MOMA exhibition *Primitivism in 20th Century Art*.

Despite a general conservatism we do see innovation in the design of British gold obverses, including the creation of elaborate swirling wreath motifs and a return to more representational stylised heads and faces (Fig. 3.3). The obverse of the Southern gold stater develops the wreath motif of the Gallo-Belgic prototype to produce a distinctive design. The hair bar of the original laureate head is still discernible, but the rest of the image is filled with a beautiful array of pellets, lines, crescents, and conjoined arcs. The Southern gold quarter stater is a very different development (possibly modelled on the coin in Fig. 2.5) with a naturalistic face, enigmatically obscured by a partial strike, together with a series of corded curls that are reminiscent of the wreath designs of the prototypes. It would be wrong to see the heads on British Celtic coins as simply reverting to the classical portrait. The head appears to have had a special place in Iron Age cultures, as the seat of spiritual power. Indeed, images of heads have been found at sacred places such as wells, springs, and lakes.

Unlike gold, British silver coins showed considerable variety and innovation. Allen believes that this is down to the absence of silver issues in the part of Gaul that influenced early British designs, while Sills attributes this to greater centralised control of gold issues in Britain. Gone are the abstractions of Apollo, and instead we see an explosion of creativity in portraying heads. We cannot know for certain whether the subject is a particular god or goddess like classical coins, but what we do know is that the range of styles is extraordinary. They are rarely just representational, incorporating abstractions as well as magical and even surreal elements. The head of the North Thames silver unit (Fig. 3.4) is a striking image, with a large, pointed nose, a semi-circular eye, and large crescents for hair, held in place by a beaded headband or diadem, and a sunburst in front. The other coin illustrated, another silver unit from the North Thames region, shares a similar line for the nose but is otherwise

Fig. 3.3. Even in the relatively conservative medium of gold, there were marvellous innovations, either developing abstract heads into elaborate wreaths or in splendid reversions to more naturalistic designs

Obverse of Southern, *Belgae, c.* 55–45 BCE, uninscribed gold stater (ABC-; Sills Hampshire British Q Derivative, dies 1/1) – Scale 1:3.2; obverse of Southern, *Regini, c.* 55–50 BCE, uninscribed gold quarter stater (ABC 551) – Scale 1:5

an altogether different style, with pin-lips, a heart-shaped ear, and a large boss on the chin.

If like the coins of the classical world, goddesses are frequently depicted on the obverse of pre-Roman British coins, we might assume that they played a major role in local traditions. However, unlike their classical counterparts, it is not always obvious which deity is being depicted leading to a lot of detective work and speculation. Another North Thames silver unit (Fig. 3.5) presents an otherworldly portrait, combining a naturalistic jaw with a linear ear-to-nose profile and swept-back corded hair. Some have looked for clues as to the identity of this image, in the earrings (female), beaded arc above the head (divinity), the sunken eye socket (all-seeing) and the floral sun (consort of sun-god, Belinus), and concluded that it is the goddess Brigit, but we simply cannot know. The other coin is East Anglian, with a female head, with a long-pointed nose, a heart-shaped ear, a lunar crown and beaded neck-torc. The snake in front (only partially revealed on this example) may indicate either the healing goddess, Sirona, or the goddess of war, Andraste. The dramatic Dio Cassius has the Icenian Queen Boudicca invoking Andraste, by revealing a hare from the folds of her clothes before her battle with Paulinus in 61 CE.

Depictions of 'goddesses' are sometimes accompanied by ducks (e.g. Fig. 3.6). Miranda Green speculates that waterfowl were considered sacred due to their ability to both swim and fly, thus connecting the worlds of life and death. The North Thames coin features a duck's head mounted on the front of a crested helmet, together with a small duck in front. In addition to possibly being another depiction of Brigit, Sills has made the intriguing suggestion that the image might be a reference to Cassivellaunos, the leader of the defence of Britain against Caesar in 54 BCE. Another duck helmet appears on a superb Southern silver unit. This image brings together many of the elements seen in previous female portraits, including an oval eye, long pointed nose, pin lips, a prominently rounded chin and spiralling locks of

Fig. 3.4. The real innovations in head depictions took place in silver units, where a vast variety of striking images were created

Obverse of North Thames, *Trinovantes*, *c.* 55–45 BCE, uninscribed silver unit (ABC 2386) – Scale 1:5; obverse of South Thames, *Berkshire, c.* 55–45 BCE, uninscribed silver unit (ABC 1007) – Scale 1:3.9

Fig. 3.5. The faces depicted on the obverse of British Celtic coins might be deities, following the classical prototype, but with highly original and sophisticated depictions

Obverse of South Thames, *Berkshire, c.* 55–40 BCE, uninscribed silver unit (ABC 1013) – Scale 1:4.6; obverse of East Anglian, *Iceni, c.* 55–50 BCE, uninscribed silver unit (ABC-; Talbot Bury A, dies E/17) – Scale 1:4.2

hair. The duck is featured hanging from a diademed helmet, with a snake, eel, or worm below its bill.

What is most distinctive about these pre-Roman British coins is their variety, innovation and artistry, rather than their subject. Another distinctive design is found on the obverse of a silver unit from Kent (Fig. 3.7). Its defining feature is a symmetrical design of two similar clean-shaven male heads, with beak-like noses, large eyes formed of ringed-pellets and line lips. The image is original even if the subject of twins is not. In Republican Rome a favourite subject was the *Dioscuri,* Castor and Pollux (the twins of Zeus), the patrons of sports, war, and general good fortune (see also Fig. 2.3). These twins were also depicted in the Janus head, such as that of the *didrachm* illustrated (also, Fig. 3.7). This model was adopted as a prototype for some Belgic coins and a bronze unit of Cunobelinus. However, the British coin is very different in design, not least because the twins are facing rather than opposed, but also because just about every other aspect of the design is different, from hair to nose to lips, together with a *bucranium* (bull's skull) below. It therefore feels appropriate that this unique coin was, in turn, adopted as the prototype for an eighth century Anglo-Saxon *sceatta*.

Roman commentators, like Caesar or Strabo, would have us believe that most of the so-called Celtic peoples of Britain were nomadic herdsmen, living off the milk and meat of their livestock. In reality they lived in settled rural communities, sowing crops and were preoccupied with fertility and the seasons. This is reflected in the imagery of two Southern silver units (Fig. 3.8). The first exudes a bounteous harvest, with corn-ears forming exuberant hair that practically eclipses the diminutive face of the corn-god. Superficially it bears some similarity to the obverse of the Gallo-Belgic Broad Flan gold stater (Fig. 1.2), given that both have big hair and diminished faces. Yet this silver unit is quite distinctive, with the presence of a corn motif and a minimalist pellet-and-line face. Fertility is also the theme of the second coin, with a 'moon-head' image, representing the lunar cycles of agriculture, sometimes associated with the female menstrual cycle. As we shall see in Chapter Six there is a

Fig. 3.6. Ducks feature on the depictions of some faces, reflecting their dual association with water and flight

Obverse of North Thames, *Trinovantes, c.* 50–40 BCE, uninscribed silver unit (ABC 2380) – Scale 1:3.9; obverse of Southern, *Regini, c.* 50–30 BCE, uninscribed silver unit (ABC-) – Scale 1:3.7

Fig. 3.7. Many societies believe that twins live under divine protection, a theme found on the Janiform head of the *dioscuri* coins of the Roman Republic, as well as this pre-Roman British coin

Obverse of Roman Republic, Anonymous Issue, Rome, *c.* 225–212 BCE, silver *didrachm* – Scale 1:2.8; obverse of Kent, *Cantiaci, c.* 50–30 BCE, uninscribed silver unit (ABC 216) – Scale 1:4.6

second face on the left, the 'nose' of which may suggest some sexual or shamanistic ritual with the main image.

We have already seen considerable variety in the techniques used to portray hair, be it tight corded curls, large crescents, spiralling locks or corn-ear exuberance. Now it is the turn of two female images that take hair to new and magical levels (Fig. 3.9). A silver unit from Kent shows elaborate hair made up of tiny seahorses or snake-scrolls. The profile is serene and probably female judging by the jewelled neck, with an oversized eye, perhaps suggesting an all-seeing deity, and an inverted sheep head in front possibly indicating a sacrifice. A different design is shown on a Southern silver unit, which has a strong lunar theme, with crescents for hair. Only four crescents are completely visible on this example, but Chris Rudd has identified up to twelve in others suggesting an entire annual cycle of perhaps the Moon herself. Both images use magical hair on female subjects to reinforce an otherworldly aspect to the images. We will now turn to hair on male subjects.

The Greek historian, Diodorus Siculus, provides some entertaining commentary on the Gallic men's hair salon, comparing their lime-washed hair to the coarseness of a horse's mane. Like Caesar, he assumes that they are clean-shaven apart from bushy moustaches, which presents challenges when eating and drinking. Two examples demonstrate the variety of British male grooming at this time (Fig. 3.10). The enigmatic East Anglian silver unit shows a completely clean-shaven man with imposing herringbone hair, a scroll-like object at the top and pellet rosette in front. Cottam and Rudd suggest that this depicts the corn-god or tree-of-life god, Esus, although we simply cannot know. The imposing North Thames coin combines lime-washed hair, a walrus moustache and a full beard (defying the Roman commentators). It has been suggested that this may be a representation of Tasciovanos himself, with the beard seeking to convey mature command. To the degree that coins reflected different fashions in male grooming, there appears to have been considerably more variety than suggested by commentators.

Fig. 3.9. British engravers took the depiction of hair to new flights of fancy, with tiny seahorses or snake-scrolls and rows of lunar crescents

Obverse of Kent, *Cantiaci, c.* 60–40 BCE, uninscribed silver unit (ABC-) – Scale 1:4.2; obverse of Southern, *Regini, c.* 50–30 BCE, uninscribed silver unit (ABC 653) – Scale 1:3.7

Fig. 3.10. British coins also depict some striking male figures, showing-off their lime-washed corded hair, elaborate herringbone hairstyles and impressive facial hair

Obverse of East Anglian, *Iceni, c.* 50–40 BCE, uninscribed silver unit (ABC 1522 var.; Talbot Large Flan A, dies D/6) – Scale 1:3.4; obverse of North Thames, *Catuvellauni, c.* 25 BCE–10 CE, uninscribed silver unit (ABC 2610) – Scale 1:3.7

Having a head, especially the head of a deity, on the obverse of a coin follows the format not only of the 'Philippus' but of most classical coins. Yet the head also had special significance for Iron Age communities, even if we do not always know who they are representing. What is most striking is the vast array of designs of heads especially on the less conservative silver, which produced distinctive and artistically creative portrayals. With a flip of a coin, we now turn to 'tails' and the depiction of horses on British Celtic coins.

4.

TAILS – BEYOND ABSTRACTION

Most British Celtic coins follow a long-established tradition of portraying horses on their 'tails' or reverse. Even if this practice dated back to the Greeks, horses obviously had a particular significance to Iron Age communities in Britain, and therefore were doubly embraced.

The Uffington White Horse on an Oxfordshire chalk hill has been dated as 500 BCE or earlier. And, while a hill is not a coin, it does illustrate the importance of the horse image in society before the import or production of coins. John Creighton has suggested that horses had both a practical and symbolic importance to regional leaders. They asserted their dominance through loyal horsemen. The horse also represented a union of ruler and land that reinforced their authority, and so was both an imported convention and something of local significance. For this reason we see the widespread adoption of the subject, combined with enormous innovation and variety in the representation of equine images.

It was not by chance that horses were prevalent on the coins of ancient Greece. According to Green, they were prestige animals associated with warrior elites, as both status symbols and tools-of-the-trade. For Anne Ross they may have also been the subject of cults, including the worship of Epona. Horses were portrayed in a variety of ways on the coins of the

Greek and Carthaginian world (Fig. 4.1). As we saw previously (Fig. 2.3), a single horse head was typically used by the Siculo-Punic Carthaginians in Sicily. A single horse, at rest or grazing, is depicted on the coins of Carthage and Larissa. Yet it is on the coins of the Greek city states of Sicily that we see some of the most spectacular horse images, whether it is a single warrior as on the *didrachm* of Gela, a two-horse (*biga*) chariot of Messana or the spectacular four-horse (*quadriga*) chariot of Syracuse.

Perhaps unsurprisingly it was the wonderful chariots of Greek coins that inspired both the Macedonian and Roman equine images (Figs 2.1 and 2.3), the former inspiring subsequent Gaulish coins, which in turn influenced British designs. The evolution of equine designs was not linear: it did not simply go from the classical representation to abstract simplifications. Instead, there were parallel developments with multiple branches and innovations, as well as reversions to earlier models. Figure 4.2 seeks to illustrate this not through a die-series, but through a schematic of ten Celtic gold coins in addition to the original Philippus, plotted by their estimated date of production against the author's subjective view of the degree of abstraction.

From the early developments of Gaulish coins based on the Macedonian prototype, discussed in Chapter Two, there is enormous innovation and development. We see progressive abstraction but also stylised developments and a reversion to naturalistic representations in the later period. There was great variety in terms of styles (lunate, disjointed, annulate), stance (standing, kneeling, rearing, prancing or galloping), mane (beaded, cabled, ladder-like, pin-cushioned, serrated or comprising S-shaped dashes), tail (single, corded, leaf-like, zig-zagged, double-stranded or triple) and much more.

British lunate horses are found exclusively on the gold staters from the North Eastern region and as their name suggests, use lunar crescents to construct the body of the horse. The inspiration for their design may be seen in the Gallo-Belgic prototype mentioned previously (Fig. 2.4),

Fig. 4.1. Horse images were very common on the coins of ancient Greece

(Clockwise from top-right)
Obverse of Sicily, Gela, *c.* 490–475 BCE, silver *didrachm* – Scale 1:1.8; obverse of Sicily, Messana, *c.* 425–421 BCE, silver *tetradrachm* – Scale 1:1.4; obverse of Sicily, Syracuse, *c.* 405–400 BCE, silver *decadrachm* – Scale 1:1.1; reverse of Siculo-Punic, Entella, *c.* 320–300 BCE, silver *tetradrachm* – Scale 1:1.4; reverse of North Africa, Carthage, *c.* 300–260 BCE, silver *shekel* – Scale 1:1.9; reverse of Thessaly, Larissa, *c.* 400–380 BCE, silver *drachm* – Scale 1:2

Fig. 4.2. The equine images of British Celtic coins show imitation of Gaulish prototypes but then multiple reinventions over time; the schematic plots eleven gold coins by their degree of abstraction (author's subjective judgement) over time, to illustrate both their variety and non-linear development

Various reverses shown, which are detailed elsewhere in Figures 2.1, 2.4, 4.3, 4.4, 8.6 and 8.8

but their British descendants evolved quite distinctively over a period of almost a century. The North Eastern gold stater is an early example (Fig. 4.3). The horse is disarticulated to create a sinuous body, with the curves of the crescents creating a sense of motion. The nose takes the form of an empty triangle or 'safety-pin', and pellets and crescents are used to indicate the charioteer above and a pelletal sun below. A much later gold stater, inscribed *Volisios Dumnocoveros* has evolved considerably. The horse assumes an almost dragon-like pose, with a large open head, horn-like pointed ears, a prominent neckline and breast, and diminutive haunches that give it the appearance of being seated. The 'dragon' theme is reinforced by the lunate lines that now resemble flames rather than convey motion.

Horse images also provide fine examples of the process which Allen described as 'disintegration' and 'abstraction' from the prototype. Even if it was neither linear nor chronological, it would be unsurprising that it was most pronounced in Britain, which was the longest-lasting producer of 'Celtic' coins. The Southern gold stater illustrated is a fine example of a disjointed or deconstructed horse (Fig. 4.4). The horse is triple-tailed, has a trefoil (three-leaf shape) under the chin and six-spoked wheel below, perhaps a legacy of the original chariot. Sills suggests that these issues may have been the work of imported engravers from Gaul, so the designs may not be entirely local. The earlier South-Western gold stater presents an even more disjointed and abstracted image of a horse. The body of the horse is reduced to pellets, the legs to sticks, the tail a 'coffee bean' and the head a 'safety-pin'. While this may be viewed as the epitome of British abstract coin imagery, Sills believes that its origins may be traced back to imported Armorican silver rather than Gallo-Belgic gold.

Another strand of development lies in annulate horses, which are constructed in part (usually at their joints) of ringed-pellets. Such coins are not unknown in Gaul but appear to be much more prevalent in British coins, with some spectacular results (Fig. 4.5). The North Thames gold quarter stater illustrated is perhaps the most impressive of

Fig. 4.3. British lunate horses are only found on the gold staters from the North-Eastern region, and, while inspired by Gaul, *Ambiani* prototypes show significant stylistic innovation

Reverse of North-Eastern, *Corieltavi, c.* 60–50 BCE, uninscribed gold stater (ABC 1719) – Scale 1:2.9; reverse of North Eastern, *Corieltavi,* Volisios Dumnocoveros, *c.* 35–40 CE, gold stater (ABC 1980) – Scale 1:2.9

BRITISH
CELTIC COINS
ART OR IMITATION?

An introduction to the coins
of pre-Roman Britain

For Madawi, Loulwa and Zyad

Fig. 4.4. The processes of disintegration and abstraction go much further in British horse images

Reverse of Southern, *Regini* & *Atrebates*, Tincomarus, *c.* 25 BCE–10 CE, gold stater (ABC 1049) – Scale 1:3.4; reverse of South-Western, *Durotriges, c.* 60–50 BCE, uninscribed gold stater (ABC 482) – Scale 1:3.1

British annulate horses. A prancing pony is created using ringed pellets, elegant lines and a stylised head. The annulate theme of the fore and hindquarters is repeated in a ringed-pellet below, an oval-pellet eye, and to a lesser extent by the 'dahlia' sun behind and a beaded ring in front. A sense of motion is created by the sprawling legs and downward tilt of the body, while the youth is conveyed by the slightly oversized head and the neat, beaded mane. The Western silver unit conveys a very different, almost mechanical impression. Double ringed-pellets form not only the fore and hindquarters but also the head. The mane is skeletal, like the connected spines of a boar-banner (Chapter 5), and the ears, legs and triple-tail are formed of curved lines. Below is a beaded ring possibly with a solar motif within, and above is what appears to be a lyre, which looks like a comb. While the lyre is probably derived from Gallic imports, the overall design is highly distinctive.

Annulate horses became increasingly sophisticated and elaborate. Two further examples illustrate both magical and naturalistic elements (Fig. 4.6). In the previous chapter, we saw two portrayals of deities with duck-heads (Fig. 3.6). The reverse of the North Thames example has an unusual annulate horse. In addition to ringed-pellets forming the body of the horse and adorning its surroundings, we also see ringed-pellets on corn ears and even a duck. The overall effect appears to celebrate or even worship the horse. A later example from the same region has a much more naturalistic horse, with a beaded mane, stick legs, a beaked mouth, and a single ringed-pellet for an eye. The annulate theme is echoed by an empty ring on the top of the head and single pellet below the raised foreleg. There is another object, possibly an acorn, below the horse.

What is most striking about the depictions of horses on British Celtic silver is the sheer variety and innovation we see. Far from being just abstractions of a naturalistic prototype, these elements are combined to create highly stylised British horse images. Another silver unit from North Thames is an innovative hybrid (Fig. 4.7). Despite a ringed-pellet eye, it does not follow the pattern of annulate horses. Instead, a naturalistic

Fig. 4.5. British annulate horses uniquely combine naturalistic and mechanical elements to produce images that range from the exquisite to the robotic

Reverse of North Thames, *Catuvellauni,* uninscribed gold quarter stater, *c.* 55–45 BCE (ABC 2466 var.; Sills dies 2/5) – Scale 1:4.6; reverse of Western, *East Wiltshire, c.* 50–40 BCE, uninscribed silver unit (ABC 2117) – Scale 1:4.6

Fig. 4.6. Annulate horses become increasingly sophisticated and elaborate, as well as increasingly naturalistic

Reverse of North Thames, *Trinovantes, c.* 50–40 BCE, uninscribed silver unit (ABC 2380) – Scale 1:3.9; reverse of North Thames, *Catuvellauni,* Tasciovanos, *c.* 25 BCE–10 CE, gold quarter stater (ABC 2586) – Scale 1:4.6

portrayal is given a 'curvy' appearance by a line threaded through the neck and body. This has the effect of reinforcing the grace of the animal but also conveys a sense of motion. It is unclear whether the large, beaded wheel above is a remnant of a chariot or a solar symbol. We have already seen the astonishing gold lunate horses from the North Eastern region (Fig. 4.3). Their portrayal of horses on silver was very different, being much more naturalistic, if stylised. The example shown (Fig. 4.7) combines stick-like legs and nose with a naturalistic body and harness. Seven pellets (only four are visible on this example) form a 'daisy' sun above the hindquarters, with the pellet motif repeated at the end of the lower jaw.

Horses were not only cult animals in their own right but also in association with gods and the sun. Ross suggests that they were seen as symbols of the sun, while Green highlights their role carrying the sky-god into battle. For this reason, the 'solar-horse' appears on both Gaulish and British Celtic coins (Fig. 4.8). One of the most vibrant of the sun-horse images is found on the reverse of a silver unit from Kent. Spring appears to be in the air in this lively image of a playful horse butting the three suns, as if to say farewell to the winter. The beaded mane emphasises the downward movement of the head and the lines from the head are either ears or moon beams indicating the passing of the night. The reverse of a Western silver unit provides a similarly playful image from a contemporary coin. It shows a triple-tailed stallion, with a beaded mane, a solar spiral above, a boar below and a neck torc in front. Like the previous coin, the overall impression is one of joyful celebration of nature coming alive. Regardless of their meaning, on which we can only speculate, solar horses represent some of the most charming equine images of pre-Roman British coins.

In Chapter Eight, we will explore the adoption of Roman imagery, including naturalistic horses, among the south-eastern 'dynasties' in the first century CE. We will end the current chapter with the more representational depictions of horses on the silver coins of the middle

Fig. 4.7. Naturalistic and abstract elements combine to create an almost infinite variety of highly stylised British horses in silver

Reverse of North Thames, *Berkshire, c.* 55–40 BCE, uninscribed silver unit (ABC 1013) – Scale 1:4.6; reverse of North Eastern, *Corieltavi, c.* 15–40 CE, uninscribed silver unit (ABC 1806) – Scale 1:3.7

Fig. 4.8. 'Solar' horses represent another innovation, celebrating the life-giving force of nature with frisky otherworldly animals

Reverse of Kent, *Cantiaci, c.* 60–40 BCE, uninscribed silver unit (ABC-) – Scale 1:4.2; reverse of Western, *East Wiltshire, c.* 50–40 BCE, uninscribed silver unit (ABC-; BMC 809) – Scale 1:3.7

of the first century BCE (Fig. 4.9). The reverse of an East Anglian silver unit provides a generally natural portrayal of a prancing horse, with tiny S-shapes for a mane and an anemone-like sun above, balanced by a pellet below. The horse held a particularly important role for the *Iceni* of this region, who are thought to have been breeders and traders. A similar composition is found on a silver unit from the Southern region, but with some important differences: the head is annulate, the mane flowing lines with pin heads, the tail is neatly corded and then appears split in two, and the hooves are clumpy and possibly back-to-front. More intriguing are the lines of tiny pellets, which may be purely decorative or represent drops of blood associated with ritual sacrifice, some evidence for which Creighton tells us comes from the Danebury Hillfort excavations.

Like the head, examined in the previous chapter, the idea of having a horse on the reverse of coins followed a classical prototype and had particular resonance for the Iron Age communities in Britain. The abstractions of Gallo-Belgic prototypes were adopted in early British gold coins, but even here there were highly distinctive and parallel developments from the stylised to the even more abstract. Unlike 'heads', there was considerable innovation on 'tails' in gold coinage as well as silver. The result is that we are left with an enormous variety of highly distinctive equine images on pre-Roman British coins. We will now explore how other animals were represented.

Fig. 4.9. Coming full circle, we see a progressive reversion to more naturalistic horse images from before the turn of the century

Reverse of East Anglian, *Iceni, c.* 50–15 BCE, uninscribed silver unit (ABC 1495 var.; Talbot Bury A, dies F/3) – Scale 1:4.6; reverse of Southern, *Belgae, c.* 50–30 BCE, uninscribed silver unit (ABC 869) – Scale 1:4.2

5.

BEASTS – BANNERS AND SPIRITS

After horses, the most frequently depicted animal on pre-Roman British coins are wild boars. If horses represented authority and light, boars were their dark, wild counterpart. Prized for their rich meat, feared for their frenzied charges and celebrated for the bravery of those who hunted them, the wild boar was clearly prized by the Iron Age Britons. Yet, like many hunting stories reality likely fell short. In popular imagination, the 'Celtic peoples of Europe' resembled Obelix, the oversized hero of Asterix the Gaul, living in a dense forest off a daily diet of wild boar joints (and, of course, some magical potion!). Even if this is the stuff of comic books, the image of Europe at the time covered in forests is deeply engrained.

For Britain, this perception has been described by Hugh Thompson as the 'Sherwood Syndrome', a deeply held view that before modern history, much of England was pristine woodland. Modernity is manifested in the form of either invaders, like the Romans and Normans, or the Industrial Revolution, either or both of which led to the demise of this idyll. This perspective is supported by classical writers, such as Strabo, who describe Britain as overgrown with forests, no doubt to reinforce the forbidding nature of this frontier province. Yet this too was a myth, given that much of England had been cleared for intensive farming as early as 1000 BCE. Research by Ralph Rowlett also suggests that the consumption of boar has been overstated, and wild animals were not a major food source in what was a developed agrarian society. Green concludes that, despite this, boar hunting was a prestige sporting activity, and its meat played a prominent role in feasting.

We must look further than hunting and feasting to understand the boar's true significance and why it is so frequently found on British Celtic coins. The boar was invoked by the local peoples as a potent symbol of war. Their ferocious and indomitable character was clearly admired, and the raised spiky bristles of an attacking boar were adopted as war motifs, including banners. They are also to be found on helmets and shields, as well as the famous *carnyx*, the war-trumpet. It has even been suggested by Simon Lilly that the boar provided inspiration for both battle tactics (charging the enemy) and even intimidating hairstyles (lime-washed hair, discussed in Chapter 3).

Yet the boar's adoption as a universal symbol in local styles of material culture, including on pre-Roman British coins, goes beyond its role as a war symbol and may reflect a broader-based cult, which saw it as a sacred animal associated with trees and burials of chieftains. Green, for example, highlights the special and complicated relationship between the 'Celts' and the creatures they hunted, involving a reverence for them and an acknowledgement that hunting was a theft from the natural world, which required appeasing rituals.

These two themes appear to be reflected in the different ways in which boars are portrayed on British Celtic coins. Some adopt a more stylised design, perhaps associated with a war banner (Fig. 5.2), while others are more naturalistic with magical or even comical elements possibly associated with a boar cult (Fig. 5.1). The 'boar-horse' series of silver coins, attributed to the *Corieltavi* 'tribe' in the North-Eastern region, is thought to have spanned around seventy years (*c.* 60 BCE–10 CE) and went through seven phases of boar portrayal, according to Matthew Rich. An early example (Fig. 5.1) portrays a loveable gangly boar, with a thin body, long legs, large curly tail, upturned snout, and prominent bristles. It is impaled by an elliptical spear and surrounded by a sun, moon and possibly stars, giving it a cosmic feel. A second example, from later in the series, is very different despite similarly long legs, with a wonderful bendy body, fearsome snout and pronounced dorsal bristles conveying a much less comical image. The lunar ringed-pellets above and below, and grassy line below the feet, suggest a portrayal in the wild. In their different ways both coins are highly distinctive representations of boars. There may well have been external influences, but the style and artistry suggest a localised development concerned with the boar as a cult figure rather than a war motif.

Banner-like representations of boars are more common across Gaul and are also found on British types, either as the primary subject or an addition to other subjects like horses (e.g. Fig. 4.8). A silver unit from the Southern region (Fig. 5.2) provides a much more stylised portrayal of a boar, with the primary emphasis on the erect bristles which are joined at their ends by a line, thus creating a war-banner motif. Above are four lunar crescents, perhaps indicating the darkness of the forests where the boars reside. Below is a snake, which may suggest re-birth or renewal (see Fig. 5.5 below). The boar itself is dripping blood, presumably following its slaughter, either through hunting or by sacrifice. Although not as common as boars, stags also held a special status for Iron Age peoples, not only as an object of hunting but also as symbols of virility and dominance of the forests. A great example is the reverse of one of the North-Eastern series, with that favoured feature of British coins, a hidden face (Chapter Six), using the stag's shaggy tail for a moustache (Fig. 6.4).

Opposing beasts are quite common in Gaulish issues but also occur in British coins with some distinctive local elements. Two Southern silver units from the middle of the first century BCE illustrate an ambiguity of subject and an originality in style not seen on their Gaulish counterparts (Fig. 5.3). The first is said to represent two back-to-back horses, but the

Fig. 5.1. After horses, boars were the most popular animal subject on British and Gaulish coins

Obverse of North-Eastern, *Corieltavi, c.* 55–45 BCE, uninscribed silver unit (ABC 1779 var.; Rich Type 6b) – Scale 1:3.7; obverse of North-Eastern, *Corieltavi, c.* 55–45 BCE, uninscribed silver unit (ABC-; Rich Type 16d var.) – Scale 1:4.2

Fig. 5.2. In both Britain and Gaul, boars were portrayed in a stylised banner-like form associated with warfare; another favoured subject conveying aristocratic bravery through hunting was the stag

Obverse of Southern, *Belgae, c.* 50–30 BCE, uninscribed silver unit (ABC 869) – Scale 1:4.2; reverse of North-Eastern, *Corieltavi, c.* 55–45 BCE, uninscribed silver unit (ABC-; Rich Type 12a) – Scale 1:4.6

absence of legs could equally convey seahorses, snakes or even dragons. It was originally thought to have been imported from Gaul, but this is countered by the discovery of multiple hidden faces (Fig. 6.1), largely absent from continental coins. The second coin with opposing beasts shares the basic format and ambiguity of the previous coin. While they look like they have the open bills of ducks, they might also be snakes or legless horses. As previously noted, ducks had a particular significance for the Iron Age communities in Britain and the Continent (Fig. 3.6), because they reflect the link between sky and water due to their ability to both fly and swim. Regardless of the subject, they present a charming picture of animals floating across the coin.

Ambiguity continues with the coins that are thought to represent dragons. Like boars, dragons may have featured on war banners as they represented leadership and strength. Two Southern silver units appear to represent dragons (Fig. 5.4). One shows a dragon-like animal with a scissor-nose and long dashes for a mane, looking back over its shoulder and breathing pellets which may represent fire. It has been suggested by Rudd that the symbol may convey the safe return from a perilous journey or military conflict, thus possibly reinforcing the idea of the dragon as a war motif. The other is a less obvious dragon, even if it has the same S-shape as the previous coin. This time the clawed beast, with what appears to be a horned head, may also be a snake (see Fig. 5.5). Three lunar crescents are visible on the left of the beast and several ringed-pellets with some beaded elements are to be found on the right. Perhaps, like the horse on the reverse, the presence of both lunar and solar elements may suggest a transition from darkness to light?

We conclude our review of beasts with snakes. We already saw in the imagery of goddesses (Fig. 3.5) that the so-called Celts, like those of Greece and Rome, associated the snake with medicine, a motif that is retained to this day for pharmacies. Green associates it with renewal, and therefore healing, due to its previously noted shedding of its skin, and its phallic shape linked with fertility. The first snake image

Fig. 5.3. Opposing beasts are quite common in Gaulish issues (e.g. Remi bronzes) but also occur in Britain with some distinctive local elements, including the presence of hidden faces (see Chapter 6)

Obverse of Southern, *Regini, c.* 55–45 BCE, uninscribed silver unit (ABC-) – Scale 1:3.4; obverse of Southern, *Regini, c.* 55–45 BCE, uninscribed silver unit (ABC 695) – Scale 1:5.5

Fig. 5.4. Dragons possibly represented leadership and strength to the so-called 'Celts' and may, like boars, have featured on military banners

Reverse of Southern, *Belgae, c.* 50–30 BCE, uninscribed silver unit (ABC-) – Scale 1:4.6; obverse of Southern, *Belgae, c.* 60–20 BCE, uniLnosrcermib eipds suimlver unit (ABC 896) – Scale 1:4.6

illustrated is a North Thames silver unit (Fig. 5.5). Here we have a long-tongued and coiled snake threatening a startled horse. The coil may either seek to mirror the ringed-pellets of the annulate horse or, according to Rudd, may convey self-renewing energy. Whatever the intended meaning, the result is a lively and distinctive image and narrative. The second, from Kent, shows a coiled dragon or snake with a segmented body, three-pronged tail and possibly horned-head. The influences for this coin may well be from Gaul, where, according to Ross, such serpents were associated with the god Cernunnos.

Unlike 'heads' and 'tails', considered in the previous two chapters, boars and other beasts were not part of the original or intermediate prototypes that initially influenced pre-Roman British coins. In a similar way to gods and horses, many animals were probably considered sacred and may even have been the focus of cults, for Iron Age communities in Britain. There were influences more from the continent than Roman prototypes, but the portrayal of naturalistic boars in particular appears to have been distinctive to British coins. We now move to consider the most British of 'innovations': mischievous hidden-faces.

Fig. 5.5. Snakes were symbols of fertility due to their phallic shape; they were also frequently horned, especially in Gallo-Roman tradition, and mistaken for dragons

Obverse of North Thames, *Eastern, c.* 50–40 BCE, uninscribed silver unit (ABC 2276) – Scale 1:3.9; obverse of Kent, *Cantiaci, c.* 50–30 BCE, uninscribed silver unit (ABC 243) – Scale 1:4.6

6.

HUMOUR – HIDDEN MISCHIEF

Hidden faces, at least on coins, appear to be mainly confined to pre-Roman Britain. Whether by accident or design, patient examination of British Celtic coins frequently reveals facial features. Some are more obvious than others, and it is possible that some of those identified might be disputed. Regardless, the phenomenon is sufficiently prevalent (occurring for example on over a tenth of the coins in my collection) that it cannot be ignored.

Over sixty years ago, the French numismatist and close friend of the surrealist André Breton, Lancelot Lengyel, identified *images cachées* on the obverse of a gold coin of the Danube. He contrasted the main image, which was representational, in profile more akin to the Greek prototype, with three further 'hidden' faces: one with a pig-like face, the other disconcerting and with a diadem, and the third a ghostly character mounting a horse. His book, *Le Secret des Celtes* aimed to decode the symbols adopted on mostly Gaulish coins.

Of course, there should be strong health warnings against over-interpreting symbols and designs for which we cannot possibly understand the context. In 1980, Allen famously highlighted the danger of trying to look behind the images on Celtic coins to discover hidden meaning. The warning was repeated thirty-seven years later by Sills, who decided to avoid interpreting designs in his epic review of Britain's gold coinage. Perhaps this risk is mitigated with respect to hidden faces, as these are images rather than symbols, so we are observing rather than interpreting. Equally, if we simply ignored them, or failed to explore their context, we would be in danger of adopting a purely 'aesthetic' approach that viewed these works of art in dangerous isolation.

When viewed in the broader context of Celtic 'art', the hidden faces we find on British coins are unsurprising. Art historians, like Ruth and Vincent Megaw, highlight the playful and ambiguous nature of designs in Celtic art, which delight in shape-changing imagery and where depictions of humans and beasts are hidden or elusive. In this respect, the art of Iron Age peoples may have been a visual expression of the oratory in which they are thought to have excelled. Simon James tells us that they delighted in an elaborate form of speaking, with plenty of allusion and circumlocution. In other words, visual tricks would be unsurprising for a society that delighted in wordplay.

When it came to coins, Van Arsdell tells us there were a lot of images within images and now-you-see-it/now-you-don'ts. The engravers seemingly loved to play with both the image itself and how it was perceived by its audience. What purpose did hidden faces play, whose faces do we see, and who decided that they should appear on coins? We can only speculate, but several not mutually exclusive suggestions have been made.

Chris Rudd has argued that these are spirit faces introduced into designs by the Druids, echoing Van Arsdell's view that the faces probably have religious significance, representing unseen forces that must be reckoned with and appeased. In a similar vein, they may be *shibboleths*, used by the artist to reference a custom or tradition of the community for whom they were made. As such, they might represent markers of loyalty or affinity, whose aim is to protect that group from actual or perceived threats.

Another interpretation is that these are signatures by the engraver. Some Greek coins were signed by their engraver (for example, the Syracuse *decadrachm* illustrated on Fig. 3.1 is signed by Euainetos, just below the lower dolphin). Might not a hidden face be the equivalent on British Celtic coins? Equally, they may be visual jokes, included playfully, with no purpose other than to entertain the engraver and those users of the coin who were in on the joke. If so, it might be viewed as an early example of British humour!

Pre-Roman British coins contain a wide range of hidden faces: glad or sad, friendly or fierce, easy to spot or hard to discern. We will start with two obvious happy faces (Fig. 6.1). The first contains multiple hidden faces on the obverse of a coin we looked at in the last chapter (Fig. 5.3). By rotating the coin 315-degrees (i.e., half-past seven on the original), we see a puckish face with a button nose and smiling mouth. At this angle, at least two further faces are visible to the left and top right. Another smiling face is to be found on the obverse of a North Thames gold quarter stater, the reverse of which we previously saw in Chapter 4 (Fig. 4.5). The highlighted face is revealed without rotation (i.e., at twelve o'clock) on this crossed-wreath motif. There are probably two further examples on this coin: one below (six o'clock), which is just peeping out of view due to the die being larger than the flan, and another is to the right (three o'clock), which is just visible and looks rather sad.

Hidden faces frequently appear to be peaking over the edge of the coin, often with a long nose protruding into the image, as if the engraver is admiring their work or having fun at our expense (Fig. 6.2). Again, we have previously seen the obverse of the first example in the context of moon-head gods of fertility (Fig. 3.8). By rotating the coin by 90-degrees, we reveal a sad little face with pronounced eyebrows, long hair, and an extended nose, looking down on the main moon-face image (at nine o'clock). One of several interpretations of the nose is that it is a phallic symbol, reinforcing the coin's theme of fertility. A similar impression is created on the Kent silver unit, which we previously saw

Fig. 6.1. Hidden faces on coins appear to be a particular innovation of pre-Roman Britain, whether formed deliberately or by accident of the design

Obverse of Southern, *Regini, c.* 55–45 BCE, uninscribed silver unit (ABC-) – Scale 1:3.4; obverse of North Thames, *Catuvellauni, c.* 55–45 BCE, uninscribed gold quarter stater (ABC 2466 var.; Sills dies 2/5) – Scale 1:4.6

in the context of twins living under divine protection (Fig. 3.7). In this case, rotating the coin by 180-degrees (from six o'clock) turns the *bucranium* of the original into an almost elephantine face, looking down on the two faces below.

What we might perceive as 'sad' faces are also revealed on British Celtic coins, some heavily disguised in intricate patterns and others in plain sight (Fig. 6.3). The wreath motifs, crescents, pellets, and lines of the obverse of the Southern gold stater have already been explored in Chapter 2 (Fig. 3.3). Even without the need for rotation, it's hard to make out the small face woven into the design (slightly up and left from six o'clock). A second, less obvious face is revealed to the right (half-past four), with linked crescents forming eyebrows and a nose. Rather simpler and more obvious is the face on another Southern example, the reverse of the coin we saw in Chapter 4 (Fig. 4.9). With minimal rotation (30-degrees) the sad face is formed of two ringed-pellets for eyes, a hoof for a nose and a downturned beaded crescent for a mouth (at five o'clock). An alternative perspective might have the beaded line ending in a single pellet (on the left) as the nose.

Finally, we have two examples of screaming or shouting faces highlighted by Rudd, where we gather the impression that a spirit is trapped in the image of the coin (Fig. 6.4). The first 'screamer' is found on the obverse of the North Thames gold stater. A rotation of 225-degrees reveals an open-mouthed face (roughly at half-past ten on the original) but also several other faces in crescents and pellets in the other quadrants. It was with respect to this series of coins that Van Arsdell admitted that it took him seven years to see the hidden face. The second shouting face is a little more complicated and perhaps debatable. It is from the reverse of the North-Eastern silver unit examined in the previous chapter (Fig. 5.2), which when rotated 210-degrees (i.e., seven o'clock on the original), reveals what may be a face. The 'eyes' are ringed-pellets, the stag's tail a 'bushy moustache' and a ringed-pellet below a 'shouting mouth'.

Fig. 6.2. Frequently, hidden faces appear to be peeking over the edge of the coin, often with a protruding nose, as if the engraver is playing some joke at our expense

Obverse of Southern, *Regini* & *Atrebates, c.* 25 BCE–10 CE, uninscribed silver unit (ABC 1049) – Scale 1:5.5; obverse of Kent, *Cantiaci, c.* 50–30 BCE, uninscribed silver unit (ABC 216) – Scale 1:4.6

Fig. 6.3. We also see sad little faces on British Celtic coins, either heavily disguised in a complex pattern or hidden in plain sight

Obverse of Southern, *Belgae, c.* 55–45 BCE, uninscribed gold stater (ABC-; Sills Hampshire British Q Derivative, dies 1/1) – Scale 1:3.2; reverse of Southern, *Belgae, c.* 50–30 BCE, uninscribed silver unit (ABC 869) – Scale 1:4.2

Fig. 6.4. It is possible to discern screaming hidden faces, which perhaps suggest someone or something trying to get out of the image

Obverse of North Thames, *Catuvellauni,* Tasciovanos, *c.* 25–10 BCE, gold stater (ABC 2565) – Scale 1:3.7; reverse of North-Eastern, *Corieltavi, c.* 55–45 BCE, uninscribed silver unit (ABC-; Rich Type 12a) – Scale 1:4.6

Whilst individual examples might be open to different interpretations or deemed accidents of complex designs, there are enough hidden faces to make the case for deliberate innovation. Their subjects, purpose and origins are harder to establish, although the idea of a visual practical joke possibly referencing the engraver is most appealing. Despite their presence on at least one continental example, they appear particularly prevalent among pre-Roman British coins, and therefore add strength to the contention that these coins were artistically original. Turning to inscriptions, it was the sponsor rather than the engraver being promoted, and through words as opposed to faces.

7.

PROPAGANDA – SELF-PROMOTION

Inscriptions and self-promotion were defining features of pre-Roman British coins during the second half of their production. By no means unique among the 'Celtic' coins from the Continent and Britain and almost certainly inspired by the Romans, this practice was more prevalent and blatant in parts of Britain than elsewhere.

Coins were used as instruments of propaganda in at least four respects: through inscriptions of the leader's name, by adding details of a leader's dynastic pedigree, using 'logos' associated with the leader and the invocation of animal imagery that referenced their name or position. This process started with Commios, who appears to have become leader of the 'tribes' in the Southern region (*Regini* and then *Atrebates*), almost certainly with Caesar's assistance and probably gold. He inscribed gold staters with his name in Latin script around 55–45 BCE, although, as Nash points out it was perhaps not until 25–15 BCE that the 'golden age' of inscribed British coins took place. This begs at least two questions: why inscribe a 'leader' rather than 'tribal' name and what prompted this development?

As we saw in Chapter One, coins have generally been assigned to the Roman *civitates* (administrative districts) in which they were found.

Thus, we have coins attributed to the *Cantiaci* in Kent, the *Durotriges* in the Western region or the *Corieltavi* in the North-Eastern region. This is obviously problematic, not least because the 'tribal' areas they represent almost certainly changed over time. An emphasis on 'tribes' is convenient albeit misleading. In Allen's view, it was the chieftain rather than tribe that issued coins from wherever they ruled. As we have seen, Sills went even further to regard the issue of gold coins in particular as a political phenomenon reflecting a leader's authority. While the role of 'leaders' and the attribution of inscriptions generally remains debatable, those of the south-east are at least corroborated by Roman sources. As we shall see in the next chapter, the later period of coin production came to be dominated by two major 'dynasties'. As they jostled for position, tribal allegiances shifted – it was the leader who became most important, and it was in their name that coins were issued.

As we noted in Chapter Two, the early prototypes adopted by Britain were Gallo-Belgic, coming from the north-eastern area of Gaul. Perhaps a sixth of the coins from this region bear inscriptions of some kind. Given that Commios came from this region, perhaps he learned the idea of inscriptions there? It is more likely that he was inspired by his early sponsor Caesar, who 'thought highly of Commius's courage and good sense'. Caesar was the absolute master of self-promotion, not least through his accounts of his campaigns in Gaul and Britain in the Gallic War.

The adoption of inscriptions by Commios's successors and their rivals probably owed more to the influence of Caesar's adopted heir – Octavian, later Augustus – than Caesar. Much debate surrounds the influence that Augustus exerted over the most prominent tribal leaders of Britain, with some like Creighton suggesting a client-state relationship, while others, like Nash, perceive a looser alliance. Less controversial is the 'soft power' Augustus exerted, and the influence it had on the iconography adopted by Britain's leaders in an effort to promote themselves through their coinage.

We start with two coins that inscribe the names of powerful leaders on their coins: Tincomarus of the Southern *Regini* and *Atrebates* and Cunobelinus of the North Thames *Trinovantes* and *Catuvellauni* (Fig. 7.1). We will hear more about Tincomarus and see the splendid reverse of his Medusa gold quarter stater in the next chapter. Here we see an unabashed 'TINC' on the obverse of the coin, blatantly promoting this Southern leader and replacing the traditional 'heads' of the coin with a Latin abbreviation for his name. Although from some years later we see a similar approach by the 'King of the Britons', Cunobelinus, who has inscribed the first three letters of his name, 'CVN', on the obverse of a silver unit. We will explore the Roman imagery adopted by Cunobelinus and others in the next chapter.

The practice of inscribing coins with the names of leaders was adopted by the leaders in the south-east from the first century CE. While this was mostly the case for gold coins as the Cunobelinus coins demonstrates, it was also done for the silver units. Inscriptions sought to reinforce the authority of the leader by including his pedigree, as we can see from two examples of leaders adding the name of their father to the inscription (Fig. 7.2). On the obverse of a Southern gold quarter stater, Verica highlights his relationship with Commios through 'COM-F'. Like Tincomarus before him, Verica claimed to be Commios's son, although, given the chronology, grandson is more likely. The Tincomarus coin (discussed previously) was also inscribed with a 'C' above and 'A' below TINC. As we will see, Epaticcus was the brother of Cunobelinus who ruled the Atrebates, and was obviously keen to stress his lineage from Tasciovanos on the obverse of his silver unit by emblazoning it with the letters 'TAS[CIO]V'. It clearly added to his credibility that his father had been the one who had built the foundations of what his brother would inherit. In addition to descent, inscriptions also emphasised to whom an issuer of coins owed their loyalty. For example, Solidus references Cunobelinus on the reverse of the Solidu coin (Fig. 7.6).

Fig. 7.1. We see more inscriptions on British Celtic coins than their Gaulish counterparts, although the idea was probably imitated from the Romans, whose alphabet was used

Obverse of Southern, *Regini* & *Atrebates*, Tincomarus, *c.* 25 BCE–10 CE, gold quarter stater (ABC 1076) – Scale 1:5.5; obverse of North Thames, *Trinovantes* & *Catuvellauni*, Cunobelinus, *c.* 9–40 CE, silver unit (ABC 2846) – Scale 1:3.9

Fig. 7.2. British leaders reinforced their legitimacy by emphasizing their pedigree

Obverse of Southern, *Regini* & *Atrebates*, Verica, *c.* 10–40 CE, silver unit (ABC 1196) – Scale 1:6.1; obverse of Southern, *Atrebates*, Epaticcus, *c.* 20–40 CE, silver unit (ABC 1349) – Scale 1:5

Self-promotion went beyond inscriptions, important though they were. Some leaders had icons, motifs, or logos they would use as a visual reminder of their authority, possibly for the benefit of those who could not read the script containing their name (Fig. 7.3). Cunobelinus employed the symbol of the corn-ear on his coins, presumably to reinforce his brand as the provider who guaranteed that his subjects would be fed. His gold quarter stater is a great example of this, together with a reference to his capital, Camulodnum ('CAMV'), now Colchester. Cunobelinus's great rival Verica was not to be outdone, and appealed to a different need through the motif of the vine leaf, suggesting that those who supported him would benefit from plenty of feasting and drinking. His gold stater is a lovely example. Other leaders may have adopted this approach, but the longevity and rivalry of Cunobelinus and Verica meant that their logos are the ones that have survived.

In a similar way, we see the dynasties of south-eastern Britain employing other visual imagery to reinforce their personal brands (Fig. 7.4). The name Cunobelinus is thought to mean the 'hound of Belenus'. Belenus was both a powerful Celtic healing god and the fabled king of the Britons according to the unreliable Geoffrey of Monmouth. The hound on the reverse of his silver unit may be a reference to Cunobelinus's cognomen, which equated to 'top dog', or perhaps even king-of-kings. Not to be outdone, Verica associated himself with the regal lion on his silver unit. And, just in case the point was not clear added 'REX'. His pitch to followers was presumably, 'if you want to have a good time feasting and drinking, align yourself with a ferocious lion as your king'.

While there is corroboration in the literature about the south-east leaders mentioned here (see Appx 5) as we saw in Chapter One, we should beware of assuming that all inscriptions are related to a chieftain or even a king. It has been suggested by Cottam and Rudd that the practice of inscribing coins was so widespread that two-thirds of the seventy 'rulers' of Britain at this time have been identified through coins. Without additional corroboration it is likely that some, if not many, of

Fig. 7.3. Self-promotion also took the form of logos or motifs associated with a particular British ruler: a corn-ear in the case of Cunobelinus and a vine leaf for Verica

Obverse of Southern, *Regini* & *Atrebates*, Verica, *c.* 10–40 CE, gold stater (ABC 1193) – Scale 1:3.2; Obverse of North Thames, *Trinovantes* & *Catuvellauni*, Cunobelinus, *c.* 8–41 CE, gold quarter stater (ABC 2822 var.; Sills Class 7c, dies 47/68) – Scale 1:5.5

Fig. 7.4. We see the dynasties of south-east Britain employing other visual images to reinforce their brand: a dog for Cunobelinus and lion for Verica

Reverse of North Thames, *Trinovantes* & *Catuvellauni*, Cunobelinus, *c.* 9–40 CE, silver unit (ABC 2846) – Scale 1:3.9; reverse of Southern, *Regini* & *Atrebates*, Verica, *c.* 10–40 CE, silver unit (ABC 1229) – Scale 1:4.2

these inscriptions describe something other than a 'ruler' in the sense we understand: for example, an elected leader, a moneyer, a place or even something unknown to us.

Yet, for the south-eastern dynasties at least, the practice of self-promotion through coins appears to have been far more developed than elsewhere among their local or Continental counterparts. As we have seen, the practice was initially adopted and then sustained by those emulating Rome. In the next chapter, we turn to consider the broader influences on the imagery of British Celtic coins.

8.

ROMANISATION – SELECTIVE ADOPTION

Allen referred to the final stage in the development of British Celtic coins as one of 'romanisation', following earlier phases of imitation, disintegration, abstraction and reintegration. This suggests that British Celtic coins had come full circle, starting with a classical Macedonian prototype and ending with a classical Roman model over a century later. In Chapter One, we explored the controversies associated with both 'art' and 'romanisation', and although these combine in the current chapter I do not propose to revisit these debates. Suffice to say that both terms are used here more narrowly (and in inverted commas) to describe originality and the adoption of Roman imagery.

With 'bookends' of imitation might we conclude that the true period of artistic innovation lay in between, perhaps with the silver issues of the second half of the first century BCE? Many would disagree, indeed, Nash refers to the 'last and most brilliant phase' of British Celtic coins starting in around 15 BCE, the very point at which Roman influences started to become most pronounced. By implication, romanisation was not incompatible with artistic merit.

The originality of 'art' may be distinguished from the 'craft' of making a faithful copy. Yet even the most innovative of art has discernible influences, and that is true of pre-Roman British coins. Roman influences in British Celtic coins were apparent from as early as the middle of the first century BCE. A striking example is the East Anglian silver unit, which appears to show a rendition of the patron goddess Roma. If we compare this image with a Roman Republican version, such as the *denarius* of M. Atilius Saranus (*c.* 148 BCE), we see that although the overall composition is broadly similar the helmets are quite distinct (Fig. 8.1). The *Iceni* helmet has something more akin to a visor while the Roman version only has a rim. The Roman helmet is winged, whereas the *Icenian* one replaces that with a curved extension of the 'visor' and a feathery motif to its left. Yet there are small details shared by both, such as the upper left line of the helmet which resolves in an ear-like loop. The British coin is a crude if imaginative 'copy' of the Roman prototype, showing less originality and craftsmanship than other silver issues of the time (e.g. Fig. 3.5). John Talbot concludes that it was adopted due to familiarity with the *denarius* through trade and even a recycling of the silver obtained from Roman coinage.

More than half a century later we see a much more overt adoption of Roman prototypes, in the form of a silver unit of Verica, which provides a higher-quality and more faithful copy of two Roman *denarii* from the previous century (Fig. 8.2). The obverse references Verica's 'father' Commios, but then lifts an image from a Mark Anthony *denarius* of 40 BCE with all the paraphernalia of a drinking celebration. The reverse prominently displays Verica's name against another borrowed image of a seated Victory, probably modelled on the Republican *denarius* of Porcia (*c.* 89 BCE). Some have suggested that Verica was a 'client king' of Rome, especially as he requested military support on the eve of the Claudian invasion. More likely, he was a beneficiary of strong trading links with Roman Gaul. Although Verica's adoption of Roman prototypes was not unique, this example is particularly blatant. Perhaps the copied superpower imagery sought to reinforce his kingly status? Alternatively, perhaps he may have simply adopted images that reinforced his victorious and feast-giving credentials?

Fig. 8.1. There is no more striking image of Rome than Roma herself, an image copied almost directly on an East Anglian coin

Obverse of Roman Republic, M. Atilius Saranus, Rome, *c.* 148 BCE, silver *denarius* – Scale 1:3.2; obverse of East Anglian, *Iceni*, *c.* 50–40 BCE, uninscribed silver unit (ABC-; Talbot Bury C, dies C/4) – Scale 1:3.9

Fig. 8.2. Britain's south-eastern dynasties from the turn of the first century CE adopted Roman prototypes

Southern, *Regini* & *Atrebates*, Verica, *c.* 10–40 CE, silver unit (ABC 1241) – Scale 1:4.6

Although the 'dynasties' of Commios (Tincomarus, Eppillus and Verica) and Tasciovanos (Cunobelinus, Epaticcus, Adminius, Caratacus, etc.) were fierce rivals in the south-east of Britain, they both used Roman imagery on their coins. We may assume that they benefited from both strong commercial and even diplomatic ties, even if they maintained their independence. Epaticcus, contemporary and rival of Verica on the south coast adopted exactly the same Roman prototype of *Victory* seated (Fig. 7.2). On the reverse is a running boar, in front of a tree with a beaded border (Fig. 8.3). It seems likely that both sides of the coins were Roman inspired. The Roman Republican *denarius*, Gens Hosidia (*c.* 68 BCE) was thought to be the inspiration for the earlier British Celtic boar images (Figs 5.1 and 5.2) but they are very different renditions. The Republican image is much closer to that on the reverse of the Epaticcus coin, which would make sense given his widespread use of other Roman imagery.

Many other British Celtic coins appear to have found their inspiration in Roman prototypes, even if they are far from being direct copies (Fig. 8.4). Another coin of Epaticcus sports an eagle which we compare with a Roman Imperial *denarius*, Petillius Capitolinus (*c.* 41 BCE). These are very different representations of eagles, and there is no suggestion that the British copied the Roman. Yet, the subject is quintessentially Roman, probably referencing a legion's *aquila* (standard). The famous East Anglian silver unit known as the 'Norfolk God' depicts a male figure wearing a boar-skin headdress, possibly to invoke the appearance or spirit of a charging boar, either for ritual or military purposes. It may have been broadly modelled on the animal headdress of the Roman Republican *denarius*, L. Roscius Fabatus (*c.* 59 BCE). A third coin is a silver minim of the celebrated Caratacus, bearing the image of the winged horse Pegasus. Despite being famous for his resistance to Roman invasion he was familiar enough with the culture to adopt the image on the *denarius,* Q. Titius (*c.* 90 BCE), and eloquent enough, according to Tacitus, to successfully defend himself in Latin in front of the emperor's tribunal when he was captured and taken to Rome.

Fig. 8.3. The Roman Republican denarius is thought to be the inspiration for the earlier British Celtic boar images (see Fig. 5.1) but appears closer to much later ones

Reverse of Roman Republic, C. Hosidi C.F. Geta III Vir, Rome, *c.* 68 BCE, silver *denarius* – Scale 1:3.2; reverse of Southern, *Atrebates*, Epaticcus, *c.* 20–40 CE, silver unit (ABC 1349) – Scale 1:5

Fig. 8.4. Many other British Celtic coins appear to have taken their inspiration from Roman prototypes, even if they are far from direct copies

(Left–right, top–bottom)
Obverse of Roman Imperatoria, Petillius Capitolinus, Rome, *c.* 41 BCE, silver *denarius* – Scale 1:2.2 – and reverse of Southern, *Atrebates*, Epaticcus, *c.* 35–43 CE, silver unit (ABC 1346) – Scale 1:3.1; obverse of Roman Republic, L. Roscius Fabatus, *c.* 59 BCE, silver *denarius* – Scale 1:2.2 – and obverse of East Anglian, *Iceni*, *c.* 20–45 CE, uninscribed silver unit (ABC 1567 var.) – Scale 1:2.9; reverse of Roman Republic, Q. Titius, Rome, *c.* 90 BCE, silver *denarius* – Scale 1:2.2 – and reverse of North Thames, *Trinovantes* & *Catuvellauni*, Caratacus, *c.* 43–51 CE, silver minim (ABC 1379) – Scale 1:5.4

While Caratacus may have been home-schooled in Latin ways, it has been suggested by Creighton that some of the earlier British leaders, like Tincomarus, may have been sent to Rome as hostages to ensure the good behaviour of those left in charge. When they returned and became coin-producing leaders, they adopted the imagery they had witnessed in their exile (Fig. 8.5). One possible example is the reverse of the fabulous 'Medusa' gold quarter stater, the obverse of which we saw in the previous chapter. There does not appear to be a Roman prototype for this image, with the closest being the Republican L. Plautius Plancus (*c.* 47 BCE), which is of a very different design and style. Creighton speculates that the inspiration came from a gorgon face decorating a shield.

As we saw in the previous chapter, coins were issued by the leader rather than the tribal group as an expression of their authority. The examples of Caratacus and Tincomarus suggest that they also expressed the cultural background of the leader.

The dynasties of south-east Britain drew inspiration from Roman themes, even if a specific prototype was not copied. There are numerous examples, but a sample will illustrate the point through the adoption of alien subjects and themes (Fig. 8.6). The silver unit of Amminus shows a hippocamp, the winged seahorse of Greek and Pheonician mythology, while the Solidus coin from Kent shows the Roman god of the sea, Neptune. Creighton believes they may both reference Augustus's victory at Actium in 31 BCE. The Cunobelinus silver unit depicts Hercules on its obverse and a woman riding a lion on its reverse. Both images are clearly Roman inspired, although we also see Cunobelinus's branding and pedigree inscribed on each side. Cunobelinus's father Tasciovanos produced wonderful gold staters in his 'Warrior' series, which combine a classical naturalistic horse with a Celtic warrior, wearing chainmail, holding a short Roman-like sword with distinctively Celtic spiky (lime-washed) hair. Another Cunobelinus coin is a hybrid, showing a stylised oak branch with nine acorns, both a significant Roman Imperial as well as possibly Druid symbol.

Fig. 8.5. Even in the absence of a clear prototype, British designs clearly take their inspiration from classical mythology

Obverse of Roman Republic, L. Plautius Plancus, Rome, *c.* 47 BCE, silver *denarius* – Scale 1:3.2; reverse of Southern, *Regini* & *Atrebates*, Tincomarus, *c.* 43–51 CE, gold quarter stater (ABC 1076) – Scale 1:5.5

Fig. 8.6. Numerous other, predominantly later types from the south-eastern dynasties incorporate Roman imagery, even if there is no obvious prototype

(Clockwise from top-right)
Reverse of Kent, *Cantiaci*, Amminus, *c.* 30–40 CE, silver unit (ABC 462) – Scale 1:3.1; reverse of Kent, *Cantiaci*, Solidus, *c.* 40–43 CE, silver unit (ABC 474) – Scale 1:3.1; obverse and reverse of North Thames, *Trinovantes & Catuvellauni*, Cunobelinus, *c.* 10–40 CE, silver unit (ABC 2864) – Scale 1:3.1; obverse of North Thames, *Catuvellauni*, Tasciovanus, *c.* 25 BCE–10 CE, gold stater (ABC 2565 var.; Sills class 5a) – Scale 1:2.5; obverse of North Thames, *Trinovantes* & *Catuvellauni*, Cunobelinus, *c.* 8–41 CE, silver unit (ABC 2906) – Scale 1:3.1

The rulers of south-east Britain wanted to portray themselves as contemporary leaders by adopting the imagery of Roman rule. The silver coin of Eppillus from Kent (Fig. 8.7), is in many ways a 'classical' coin. On the obverse there is a laureate head not unlike an Apollo, and on the reverse a naturalistic warrior holding a *carnyx*. Both sides of this coin have Roman themes and even if they are not directly attributable to a Roman prototype, the obverse bears some similarity to the Republican *denarius*, L. Memmius (*c.* 109–108 BCE). Van Arsdell has suggested that this coin was a celebration of some short-lived victories and was produced to finance military operations against Cunobelinus.

We see the adoption of Roman imagery together with local elements, including the prominently inscribed name of Eppillus on both sides, and the incorporation of the Celtic war-trumpet, *carnyx*, discussed previously in Chapter 5. While not as blatant as his 'nephew' Verica, Eppillus appears to be promoting himself as 'king' of the *Cantiaci* and possibly *Atrebates* by adopting the portraiture of a Roman leader.

Our final coin is appropriately from Cunobelinus (Fig. 8.8), who Suetonius referred to as the 'king of the Britons' and certainly appears to have ruled or had control of the largest and most prosperous parts of Britain. Rome was on his doorstep in Gaul, and the adjacent lands of Cunobelinus according to Strabo benefited from a healthy exportation of grain, cattle, metals, hides, dogs and slaves. There is archaeological evidence for the gruesome trade in people, including chains and manacles from the period.

While more Jacobean romp than historical narrative, Shakespeare's Cymbeline (modelled on Cunobelinus) captures the ambiguity of the connected-yet-independent relationship with Rome, although for dramatic effect the play paints a more polarised picture of a vassal state rebelling. The Cunobelinus gold stater bears his characteristic corn-ear motif and references his capital, the reverse depicting an Augustan Roman horse with his name above it. It is another hybrid,

Fig. 8.7. The rulers of the south-eastern dynasties sought to portray themselves as contemporary leaders, adopting the imagery of Roman role models

Kent, *Cantiaci*, Eppillus, *c.* 1–15 CE, silver unit (ABC 399) – Scale 1:3.7

with the local ruler's logo and branding on the obverse and Roman imagery on the reverse.

It is tempting to interpret this final period of British Celtic coins as one during which Rome achieved a cultural conquest before their physical one, akin to the original conception of 'Romanisation'. From those leaders closest to the continent in south-east Britain, there was wholesale adoption of Roman prototypes and iconography. It is possible that many of the leaders received a Roman education either at home or as hostages. Latin was adopted as the language of their coins, and there were close commercial and even diplomatic ties with the Roman continent. Yet the idea of a cultural conquest, like the suggestion the southern Kingdoms were client states, appears to go too far. These alien symbols and images were combined with local themes as well as the branding and inscription of the ruler themselves. The coins of this time reflect a balancing act by those in power to maintain connections as well as their independence. Only this can explain why Rome experienced so much resistance when it sought to conquer Britain.

Fig. 8.8. Cunobelinus was undoubtedly the most powerful ‘King of the Britons’, who incorporated Roman features in his coins

North Thames, *Trinovantes* & *Catuvellauni*, Cunobelinus, *c.* 8–41 CE, gold stater (ABC 2774) – Scale 1:3.4

CONCLUSIONS

There is both Art and Imitation in British Celtic coins. The balance of originality and replication varies enormously by time, authority, region and even coin type. Some are direct copies of Gaulish or Roman coins, many have incorporated 'foreign' imagery or subject matter, and most reflect the format of Macedonian or Greek prototypes. There is also enormous variety and innovation, with greater levels of abstraction, stylised hybrids, intricate designs with hidden faces and an unprecedented level of self-promotion by dynastic leaders. Some coins are little more than replicas while others are entirely original, and in between we see a unique blend of external influences and local innovations.

In the second chapter, Origins, we saw that there were prototypes that formed the basis of early pre-Roman British coins. These were Gallo-Belgic with origins in Macedonian prototypes. Yet, we also saw that even the Macedonian 'Philippus' was probably modelled on the coins of a neighbouring group Philip II had conquered. Moreover there were multiple prototypes adopted in the coinages of Iron Age peoples across the continent. Roman coins, which were to exert an influence on British Celtic coins, had their own influences from the Greek city states of *Magna Graecia*.

In the third, fourth and fifth chapters, we saw the explosion of creativity on the back of the basic format and designs of early British coins. The adoption of a 'head' on the obverse of coins, potentially portraying a deity, did not stop extraordinary innovation in the way that Celtic or British gods and goddesses were portrayed particularly in the less conservative medium of silver. 'Tails' or horses were adopted as the dominant theme on the reverse of coins, and while the disintegrated Gallo-Belgic prototype was used initially, there were numerous different strands of development in equine images. Other animals, most importantly the boar, were also portrayed on the silver coins of this period creating a range of stylised, abstract, and magical images.

The sixth and seventh chapters explored the British development of hidden faces and the unprecedented self-promotion of leaders. Largely confined to British coins, a variety of faces (some more cheerful than others) are to be found upon careful inspection of coins. Whether these had a religious purpose, they may also form the British equivalent of the engraver's signature. Inscriptions were not new and almost certainly copied from Roman coins, but then we see them going to new levels, citing the pedigree of a ruler and adopting a logo or brand. Both were particularly prevalent in pre-Roman British coins.

Finally in the eighth chapter, we appear to come full circle, from classical Macedonian influences at the beginning to classical Roman ones at the end. Like the suggestion that the south-eastern dynasties were client or vassal-states of Rome, it is almost certainly wrong to see their adoption of Roman imagery as suggesting of a cultural subservience. Rather, it was more likely a reflection of close commercial and diplomatic ties, and the balancing act of maintaining friendly but independent relations with a powerful neighbour.

The story of pre-Roman British coins is more nuanced than the *Art or Imitation* theme suggests. Given the variety of styles and types, it is impossible to give a simple yes or no to the implied question. It is tempting to say there was more imitation (of Gaulish coins) in the early period, more innovation in between (especially in silver) and a reversion to imitation (of Roman designs) latterly. Yet this is also an over-simplification as there were many exceptions to this rule. Equally, we may suggest that particular 'tribes' or 'leaders' were more imitative than others with the dynasties of the south-east being prime examples. This too misses the point that some of the other tribes stopped innovating even if they did not adopt Roman themes, and the dynasties themselves launched unprecedented levels of self-promotion.

The rich variety of pre-Roman British coins is matched by the controversies summarised in the first chapter. Debates continue about the identity of those who produced and used these coins, how they came to adopt coinage and for what purpose, and how original their designs were. For many, we should not use the word 'art' to describe them or 'romanisation' to describe their later influences. Yet, it is this very variety, blending of influences, and passionate controversy that makes these coins so worthy of collection and study.

COINS ILLUSTRATED

Front cover: obverse of Southern, *Regini*, *c.* 50–30 BCE, uninscribed silver unit, (ABC-)

Back cover: reverse of North Thames, *Catuvellauni*, *c.* 55–45 BCE, uninscribed gold quarter stater, (ABC 2466 var.; Sills dies 2/5)

Fig. 1.2. Gallo-Belgic, *Bellovaci*, *c* 150-125 BCE, 'Broad Flan' uninscribed gold stater (ABC 4)

Fig. 2.1. Kings of Macedon, Philip II or Alexander III, Pella, *c.* 340/36–328 BCE, gold stater

Fig. 2.2. Kings of Macedon, Pella, Philip II, *c* 336/5-329/8 BCE, silver tetradrachm; Kings of Macedon, Alexander III, Amphipolis, *c.* 323–320 BCE, silver *tetradrachm*; Gaul, Massalia, *c.* 125–90 BCE, silver *drachm*

Fig. 2.3. Roman Republic, Anonymous Issue, Romano-Campanian, *c.* 240 BCE, silver *didrachm*; Roman Republic, L. Saufeius, Rome, *c.* 152 BCE, silver *denarius*; Roman Republic, C. Terentius Lucanus, Rome, *c.* 147 BCE, silver *denarius*

Fig. 2.4. Reverse of Gaul, *Eburovices*, *c.* 75–50 BCE, gold half stater (Scheers Class 3: LT 7019 var.); reverse of Gaul, *Ambiani*, *c.* 50 BCE, gold stater (ABC 16)

Fig. 2.5. Obverse of Gaul, *Coriosolites*, *c.* 57–56 BCE, silver stater (ABC 70); obverse of South Western, *Durotriges*, *c.* 50–30 BCE, uninscribed gold quarter stater (ABC 2205)

Fig. 2.6. Britain, Elizabeth II, 2013, gold sovereign

Fig. 3.1. Reverse of Sicily, Leontini, *c.* 450–440 BCE, silver *tetradrachm*; obverse of Attica, Athens, *c.* 510–490 BCE, silver *drachm*; reverse of Sicily, Syracuse, *c.* 405–400 BCE, silver *decadrachm*; obverse of Lokris, Lokri Opuntii, *c.* 340 BCE, silver *stater*; obverse of North Africa, Carthage, *c.* 300–260 BCE, silver *shekel*; obverse of Carthage, Second Punic War, *c.* 220–205 BCE, silver half *shekel*

Fig. 3.2. Obverse of North Eastern, *Corieltavi*, *c.* 60–50 BCE, uninscribed gold stater (ABC 1719); obverse of South Western, *Durotriges*, *c.* 58–45 BCE, uninscribed silver stater (ABC 2163)

Fig. 3.3. Obverse of Southern, *Belgae*, *c.* 55–45 BCE, uninscribed gold stater (ABC-; Sills Hampshire British Q Derivative, dies 1/1); obverse of Southern, *Regini*, *c.* 55–50 BCE, uninscribed gold quarter stater (ABC 551)

Fig. 3.4. Obverse of North Thames, *Trinovantes*, *c.* 55–45 BCE, uninscribed silver unit (ABC 2386); obverse of North Thames, *Berkshire*, *c.* 55–45 BCE, uninscribed silver unit (ABC 1007)

Fig. 3.5. Obverse of North Thames, *Berkshire*, *c.* 55–40 BCE, uninscribed silver unit (ABC 1013); obverse of East Anglian, *Iceni*, *c.* 55–50 BCE, uninscribed silver unit (ABC-; Talbot Bury A, dies E/17)

Fig. 3.6. Obverse of North Thames, *Trinovantes*, *c.* 50–40 BCE, uninscribed silver unit (ABC 2380); Obverse of Southern, *Regini*, *c.* 50–30 BCE, uninscribed silver unit (ABC-)

Fig. 3.7. Obverse of Roman Republic, Anonymous Issue, Rome, *c.* 225–212 BCE, silver *didrachm*; obverse of Kent, *Cantiaci*, *c.* 50–30 BCE, uninscribed silver unit (ABC 216)

Fig. 3.8. Obverse of Southern, *Regini*, *c.* 55–45 BCE, uninscribed silver unit (ABC 659); obverse of Southern, *Regini* & *Atrebates*, *c.* 50–25 BCE, uninscribed silver unit (ABC 1034)

Fig. 3.9. Obverse of Kent, *Cantiaci*, *c.* 60–40 BCE, uninscribed silver unit (ABC-); obverse of Southern, *Regini*, *c.* 50–30 BCE, uninscribed silver unit (ABC 653)

Fig. 3.10. Obverse of East Anglian, *Iceni*, *c.* 50–40 BCE, uninscribed silver unit (ABC 1522 var.; Talbot Large Flan A, dies D/6); obverse of North Thames, *Catuvellauni*, *c.* 25 BCE–10 CE, uninscribed silver unit (ABC 2610)

Fig. 4.1. Obverse of Sicily, Gela, *c.* 490–475 BCE, silver *didrachm*; obverse of Sicily, Messana, *c.* 425–421 BCE, silver *tetradrachm*; obverse of Sicily, Syracuse, *c.* 405–400 BCE, silver *decadrachm*; reverse of Siculo-Punic, Entella, *c.* 320–300 BCE, silver *tetradrachm*; reverse of North Africa, Carthage, *c.* 300–260 BCE, silver *shekel*; reverse of Thessaly, Larissa, *c.* 400–380 BCE, silver *drachm*

Fig. 4.2. Various reverses shown, which are detailed elsewhere in Figures 2.1, 2.4, 4.3, 4.4 and 8.8

Fig. 4.3. Reverse of North Eastern, *Corieltavi*, *c.* 60–50 BCE, uninscribed gold stater (ABC 1719); reverse of North Eastern, *Corieltavi*, Volisios Dumnocoveros, *c.* 35–40 CE, gold stater (ABC 1980);

Fig. 4.4. Reverse of Southern, *Regini* & *Atrebates*, Tincomarus, *c.* 25 BCE–10 CE, gold stater (ABC 1049); reverse of South Western, *Durotriges*, *c.* 60–50 BCE, uninscribed gold stater (ABC 482)

Fig. 4.5. Reverse of North Thames, *Catuvellauni* uninscribed gold quarter stater, *c.* 55–45 BCE (ABC 2466 var.; Sills dies 2/5); reverse of Western, *East Wiltshire*, *c.* 50–40 BCE, uninscribed silver unit (ABC 2117)

Fig. 4.6. Reverse of North Thames, *Trinovantes*, *c.* 50–40 BCE, uninscribed silver unit (ABC 2380); reverse of North Thames, *Catuvellauni*, Tasciovanos, *c.* 25 BCE–10 CE, gold quarter stater (ABC 2586)

Fig. 4.7. Reverse of North Thames, *Berkshire*, *c.* 55–40 BCE, uninscribed silver unit (ABC 1013); reverse of North Eastern, *Corieltavi*, *c.* 15–40 CE, uninscribed silver unit (ABC 1806)

Fig. 4.8. Reverse of Kent, *Cantiaci*, *c.* 60–40 BCE, uninscribed silver unit (ABC-); reverse of Western, *East Wiltshire*, *c.* 50–40 BCE, uninscribed silver unit (ABC-; BMC 809)

Fig. 4.9. Reverse of East Anglian, *Iceni*, *c.* 50–15 BCE, uninscribed silver unit (ABC 1495 var. Talbot Bury A, dies F/3); reverse of Southern, *Belgae*, *c.* 50–30 BCE, uninscribed silver unit (ABC 869)

Fig. 5.1. Obverse of North Eastern, *Corieltavi*, *c.* 55–45 BCE, uninscribed silver unit (ABC 1779 var.; Rich Type 6b); obverse of North Eastern, *Corieltavi*, *c.* 55–45 BCE, uninscribed silver unit (ABC-; Rich Type 16d var.)

Fig. 5.2. Obverse of Southern, *Belgae*, *c.* 50–30 BCE, uninscribed silver unit (ABC 869); reverse of North Eastern, *Corieltavi*, *c.* 55–45 BCE, uninscribed silver unit (ABC-; Rich Type 12a)

Fig. 5.3. Obverse of Southern, *Regini*, *c.* 55–45 BCE, uninscribed silver unit (ABC-); obverse of Southern, *Regini*, *c.* 55–45 BCE, uninscribed silver unit (ABC 695)

Fig. 5.4. Reverse of Southern, *Belgae*, *c.* 50–30 BCE, uninscribed silver unit (ABC-); obverse of Southern, *Belgae*, *c.* 60–20 BCE, uninscribed silver unit (ABC 896)

Fig. 5.5. Obverse of North Thames, *Eastern*, *c.* 50–40 BCE, uninscribed silver unit (ABC 2276); obverse of Kent, *Cantiaci*, *c.* 50–30 BCE, uninscribed silver unit (ABC 243)

Fig. 6.1. Obverse of Southern, *Regini*, *c.* 55–45 BCE, uninscribed silver unit (ABC-); obverse of North Thames, *Catuvellauni*, *c.* 55–45 BCE, uninscribed gold quarter stater (ABC 2466 var.; Sills dies 2/5)

Fig. 6.2. Obverse of Southern, *Regini* & *Atrebates*, *c.* 25 BCE–10 CE, uninscribed silver unit (ABC 1049); obverse of Kent, *Cantiaci*, *c.* 50–30 BCE, uninscribed silver unit (ABC 216)

Fig. 6.3. Obverse of Southern, *Belgae*, *c.* 55–45 BCE, uninscribed gold stater (ABC-; Sills Hampshire British Q Derivative, dies 1/1); reverse of Southern, *Belgae*, *c.* 50–30 BCE, uninscribed silver unit (ABC 869)

Fig. 6.4. Obverse of North Thames, *Catuvellauni*, Tasciovanos, *c.* 25–10 BCE, gold stater (ABC 2565); reverse of North Eastern, *Corieltavi*, *c.* 55–45 BCE, uninscribed silver unit (ABC-; Rich Type 12a)

Fig. 7.1. Obverse of Southern, *Regini* & *Atrebates*, Tincomarus, *c.* 25 BCE–10 CE, gold quarter stater (ABC 1076); obverse of North Thames, *Trinovantes* & *Catuvellauni*, Cunobelinus, *c.* 9–40 CE, silver unit (ABC 2846)

Fig. 7.2. Obverse of Southern, *Regini* & *Atrebates*, Verica, *c.* 10–40 CE, silver unit (ABC 1196); obverse of Southern, *Atrebates*, Epaticcus, *c.* 20–40 CE, silver unit (ABC 1349)

Fig. 7.3. Obverse of North Thames, *Trinovantes* & *Catuvellauni*, Cunobelinus, *c.* 8–41 CE, gold quarter stater (ABC 2822 var.; Sills Class 7c, dies 47/68); obverse of Southern, *Regini* & *Atrebates*, Verica, *c.* 10–40 CE, gold stater (ABC 1193)

Fig. 7.4. Reverse of North Thames, *Trinovantes* & *Catuvellauni*, Cunobelinus, *c.* 9–40 CE, silver unit (ABC 2846); reverse of Southern, *Regini* & *Atrebates*, Verica, *c.* 10–40 CE, silver unit (ABC 1229)

Fig. 8.1. Obverse of Roman Republic, M. Atilius Saranus, Rome, *c.* 148 BCE, silver *denarius*; obverse of East Anglian, *Iceni*, *c.* 50–40 BCE, uninscribed silver unit (ABC-; Talbot Bury C, dies C/4)

Fig. 8.2. Southern, *Regini* & *Atrebates*, Verica, *c.* 10–40 CE, silver unit (ABC 1241)

Fig. 8.3. Reverse of Roman Republic, C. Hosidi C.F. Geta III Vir, Rome, *c.* 68 BCE, silver *denarius*; reverse of Southern, *Atrebates*, Epaticcus, *c.* 20–40 CE, silver unit (ABC 1349)

Fig. 8.4. Obverse of Roman Imperatoria, Petillius Capitolinus, Rome, *c.* 41 BCE, silver *denarius* and reverse of Southern, *Atrebates*, Epaticcus, *c.* 35–43 CE, silver unit (ABC 1346); obverse of Roman Republic, L. Roscius Fabatus, *c.* 59 BCE, silver *denarius* and obverse of East Anglian, *Iceni*, *c.* 20–45 CE, uninscribed silver unit (ABC 1567 var.); reverse of Roman Republic, Q. Titius, Rome, *c* 90 BCE, silver *denarius* and reverse of North Thames, *Trinovantes* & *Catuvellauni*, Caratacus, *c.* 43–51 CE, silver minim (ABC 1379)

Fig. 8.5. Obverse of Roman Republic, L. Plautius Plancus, Rome, *c.* 47 BCE, silver *denarius*; reverse of Southern, *Regini* & *Atrebates*, Tincomarus, *c.* 43–51 CE, gold quarter stater (ABC 1076)

Fig. 8.6. Reverse of Kent, *Cantiaci*, Amminus, *c.* 30–40 CE, silver unit (ABC 462); reverse of Kent, *Cantiaci*, Solidus, *c.* 40–43 CE, silver unit (ABC 474); obverse and reverse of North Thames, *Trinovantes* & *Catuvellauni*, Cunobelinus, *c.* 10–40 CE, silver unit (ABC 2864); obverse of North Thames, *Catuvellauni*, Tasciovanus, *c.* 25 BCE–10 CE, gold stater (ABC 2565 var.; Sills class 5a); obverse of North Thames, *Trinovantes* & *Catuvellauni*, Cunobelinus, *c.* 8–41 CE, silver unit (ABC 2906)

Fig. 8.7. Kent, *Cantiaci*, Eppillus, *c.* 1–15 CE, silver unit (ABC 399)

Fig. 8.8. North Thames, *Trinovantes* & *Catuvellauni*, Cunobelinus, *c.* 8–41 CE, gold stater (ABC 2774)

APPENDICES

Appendix 1. Glossary

General Terms

Die	engraved piece with the design for stamping the coin
Exergue	part of design in which the legend is placed
Flan/Blank	blank metal piece before striking
Legend	principal inscription on a coin
Numismatics	the study or collection of coins
Obverse	front side of a coin ('heads')
Patina	surface film caused by oxidation (Cabinet Tone)
Reverse	back side of a coin ('tails')
Strike	sharpness of the detail on the coin's original design
Type	a coin's basic distinguishing design

Denominations

A variety of denominations have been adopted, broadly from the classical world. Of course, we cannot know how those who produced or used these coins described them, but we do know that their production followed broad denominational themes of size, weight and primary metal (note: the sizes and weights quoted are averages based on the authors own unrepresentative collection and should therefore be considered as indications only).

Gold Denominations	The primary denominations of gold coins were the 'stater' (*c.* 16–17 mm diameter; *c.* 5.55 g weight) and 'quarter stater' (*c.* 10–11 mm; *c.* 1.22 g); imported coins included Gallo-Belgics, like the 'broad flan stater' which was a little larger (*c.* 24 mm).

Silver Denominations	There were a variety of silver denominations, including larger 'staters' or 'billions' (a little larger than gold staters but of a similar or lighter weight), but the primary denomination was the silver 'unit' (*c.* 12–13 mm; *c.* 1.15 g but with significant variation) and its diminutive 'minim' (*c.* 7–8 mm; *c.* 0.25 g).
Bronze Denominations	Bronze coins were also present, again in a range of denominations, but principally in the form of 'units', be they single (*c.* 15 mm; *c.* 1.90 g), double or half; it is debatable whether 'potins' were a subset of bronze or a denomination in their own right (*c.* 18 mm; *c.* 1.99 g).

Coin Regions

Coins are quite commonly ascribed to a 'tribal' area, derived from the Roman *civitas* (administrative districts). This is debatable in the absence of reliable contemporary accounts and because coin production preceded Roman administration. For this reason, coin-producing regions have been described in geographic rather than tribal terms. What follows is a reconciliation of the two (see also Appx 4).

South-Western	*Durotriges*
Western	*Dobunni* and *East Wiltshire*
Southern	*Atrebates*, *Regini*, *Belgae* and *Berkshire*
Kent	*Cantiaci*
North Thames	*Catuvellauni* and *Trinovantes*
East Anglian	*Iceni*
North-Eastern	*Corieltavi*

Appendix 2. Early Timeline

CENTURY	CLASSICAL WORLD	'CELTIC' WORLD
5th BCE	Persian Wars (Greeks repel Persians)	Hallstatt period (Early Iron Age cultural centres)
	Peloponnesian War (Sparta defeats Athens)	La Tène period (Middle to Late Iron Age, first Greek mention of Celts)
4th BCE		Celts increase in Po Valley, Gauls take Rome
		Celtic mercenaries in Greece
	Philip II of Macedon (conquests in Greece)	
	Alexander III 'The Great' (conquests reach India)	Celts meet with Alexander

CENTURY	CLASSICAL WORLD	'CELTIC' WORLD
3rd BCE	Samnite Wars (Rome expands control in Italy)	
	Pyrrhic War (Rome repels Greek invader, wins Tarentum)	Senones defeated by Rome Celts sack Delphi, some migrate to Asia Minor (Galatia)
	First Punic War (Rome gains Sicily)	
	Second Punic War (Rome defeats Carthage, gains Spain)	Celts of Northern Italy (Cisalpine Gauls) defeated by Rome
2nd BCE	Macedonian Wars (Rome gains Greece)	
	Third Punic War (Rome defeats and destroys Carthage)	
		Celts in southern Gaul annexed by Rome

(after Cunliffe 2018, Table 1, 426–7)

Appendix 3. Later Timeline

CENTURY	CLASSICAL WORLD	'CELTIC' WORLD
1st BCE	Social War (Roman allies in Italy rebel) Sulla dictatorship First Triumvirate (Pompey, Caesar & Crassus) Civil War and assassination of Caesar Second Triumvirate (Octavian, Anthony & Lepidus) Battle of Actium (Octavian defeats Anthony) Octavian named Emperor Augustus Cantabrian Wars (Romans defeat Iberian tribes) Germanic Wars (Romans cross the Rhine)	Eastern Celts defeated (by Dacians) Gallic Wars (Caesar) Caesar invades Britain (twice) and crosses Rhine Unsuccessful uprisings against Roman occupation (Gaul) Commios (leader of Atrebates, retreats to Britain, achieves dominance south of Thames)

CENTURY	CLASSICAL WORLD	'CELTIC' WORLD
1st CE	Romans defeated by Germanic tribes (Teutoburg Forest) Tiberius succeeds Augustus on his death	Cunobelinus ('King of the Britons') north of Thames; Verica 'King' in the south
	Caligula succeeds Tiberius on his death Claudius succeeds Caligula on his assassination	
		Conquest of Britain (Plautius) Caratacus, son of Cunobelinus, captured, tried and freed (Rome)
	Nero succeeds Claudius on his death Galba succeeds Nero after he is deposed Year of the 'Four Emperors' (Galba, Vitellius, Otho & Vespasian)	Rebellion of Boudica and her defeat (Paulinus)
	Titus succeeds his father Vespasian on his death Domitian succeeds his elder brother, Titus, on his death	Campaign in Scotland (Agricola)
	Nerva succeeds Domitian who is assassinated Trajan succeeds Nerva on his death	

(after Cunliffe 2018, Table 1, 426–7)

Appendix 4. Evolution of pre-Roman British Coin Classifications

<table>
<tr><th rowspan="2">Evans (1864)</th><th rowspan="2">Mack (1953)</th><th rowspan="2">Allen (1960)</th><th rowspan="2">Haselgrove (1987)</th><th rowspan="2">Van Arsdell (1989)</th><th rowspan="2">Hobbs (1996)</th><th colspan="2">Cottam et al. (2010)</th><th>Leins (2012)</th></tr>
<tr><th>Regions</th><th>'Tribal Groups'</th><th></th></tr>
<tr><td rowspan="2">Unin-scribed</td><td></td><td>Uninscribed</td><td>–</td><td>–</td><td>Early Un-inscribed</td><td></td><td>–</td><td>–</td></tr>
<tr><td>Durotriges</td><td>Durotriges</td><td>South-Western</td><td>Durotriges</td><td>South-Western</td><td>South-Western</td><td>Durotriges</td><td>South-Western</td></tr>
<tr><td rowspan="2">Western</td><td rowspan="2">Dobunni</td><td rowspan="2">Dobunni</td><td rowspan="2">Western</td><td rowspan="2">Dobunni</td><td rowspan="2">Western</td><td rowspan="2">Western</td><td>Dobunni</td><td rowspan="2">Western (inc. E Wilts)</td></tr>
<tr><td>East Wiltshire</td></tr>
<tr><td rowspan="5">South-Eastern</td><td rowspan="5">Atrebates & Regni</td><td rowspan="5">Atrebates</td><td rowspan="5">Southern</td><td rowspan="5">Atrebates</td><td rowspan="5">Southern</td><td rowspan="5">Southern</td><td>Atrebates</td><td rowspan="5">Southern (inc. Berks)</td></tr>
<tr><td>'Vectuarii'</td></tr>
<tr><td>'Regini'</td></tr>
<tr><td>Belgae</td></tr>
<tr><td>Berkshire</td></tr>
<tr><td>Kentish</td><td>Cantii</td><td>Cantii</td><td>South-Eastern</td><td>Cantii</td><td>South-Eastern</td><td>Kent</td><td>'Cantiaci'</td><td>Kentish</td></tr>
<tr><td rowspan="2">Central</td><td>Catuvel-launi</td><td rowspan="2">Trinovantes</td><td rowspan="2">Eastern</td><td rowspan="2">Trinov-antes</td><td rowspan="2">Northern</td><td rowspan="2">North Thames</td><td>Catuvel-launi</td><td rowspan="2">Eastern</td></tr>
<tr><td>Trinovantes</td><td>Trinovantes</td></tr>
<tr><td>Eastern</td><td>Iceni</td><td>Iceni</td><td>East Anglia</td><td>Iceni</td><td>East Anglia</td><td>East Anglian</td><td>Iceni</td><td>East Anglia</td></tr>
<tr><td>Yorkshire</td><td>Brigantes</td><td>'Coritani'</td><td>North-Eastern</td><td>'Coriel-tauvi'</td><td>North-Eastern</td><td>North-Eastern</td><td>Corieltavi</td><td>North-Eastern</td></tr>
</table>

(after Leins 2012, Table 3.1, 37)

Appendix 5. 'Tribes' and Inscribed 'Authorities' on pre-Roman British Coins

REGION	CIVITAS ('Tribal Group')	COIN INSCRIPTIONS ('Authorities')			
		pre-*c.* 25 BCE	*c.* 25 BCE–1 CE	*c.* 1–20 CE	post-*c.* 20 CE
KENT	Cantiaci		**Dubnovellau-nos** Vosenos	Sam, Eppillus, Touto, **Verica,** Sego	**Cunobelinus** **Amminius** Solidus
SOUTHERN	Atrebates	**Commios**	**Tincomaros** Eppillus	**Verica**	**Verica** Epaticcus **Caratacus**
	Regini				
	Belgae				
	Vectuarii			Crab	
	Berkshire				
EAST ANGLIA	Iceni			Cani Duro	Antedios, Ecen Saenu/Saeviu Aesu Ale or Al fe Scavo Esuprastus/Esico
NORTH-EASTERN	Corieltavi			Cat Vepo	Vepo, Aunt Covat Dumnocoveros Tigirseno Esuprasu, Lat Ison Volisios Cartivellaunos Dumnovellaunos
WESTERN	Dobunni		Corio Boduoc	Comux Catti Inamn	Anted Eisu
	East Wiltshire				
SOUTH-WESTERN	Durotriges				
NORTH THAMES	Catuvellauni	Addedomaros	Tasciovanos Andoco	**Cunobelinus** Diassu, Rues, Trocc	**Cunobelinus** Agr
	Trinovantes	Addedomaros	**Dubnovel-launos**		

Sources: Where inscribed authorities are mentioned in classical sources, they have been highlighted in bold: Caesar (Commios); Augustus (Dubnovellaunos, Tincomarus); Tacitus (Caratacus); Suetonius (Amminus, Cunobelinus); Dio Cassius (Caratacus, Cunobelinus, Verica)

BIBLIOGRAPHY

Aldhouse-Green, M.J. 1992. *Dictionary of Celtic Myth and Legend*. London: Thames and Hudson

Aldhouse-Green, M.J. 1993. *Celtic Myths*. London: British Museum Press

Allen, D.F. 1978. *An Introduction to Celtic Coins*. London: British Museum

Allen, D.F. and Nash, D. (ed). 1980. *The Coins of the Ancient Celts*. Edinburgh: University Press

Collis, J. 2010. *The Celts: Origins, myths & inventions*. Stroud: Tempus

Cottam, E. 2022. *Coins of the Iceni*. Aylsham: Chris Rudd

Cottam, E. and Rudd, C. 2013. *Britain's First Coins*. Aylsham: Chris Rudd

Cottam, E., de Jersey, P., Rudd, C. & Sills, J. 2010. *Ancient British Coins*. Aylsham: Chris Rudd

Crawford, M. 1974. *Roman Republican Coinage*. London: Cambridge University Press

Creighton, J. 2000. *Coins and Power in Late Iron Age Britain*. Cambridge: Cambridge University Press

Cunliffe, B. 2001. *The Extraordinary Voyage of Pytheas the Greek*. London: Allen Lane

Cunliffe, B. 2005. *Iron Age Communities in Britain: An account of England, Scotland and Wales from the seventh century BC until the Roman conquest*. 4th edn. London: Routledge

Cunliffe, B. 2018. *The Ancient Celts*. Oxford: Oxford University Press

Cunliffe, B. & Koch, J.T. 2019. *Exploring Celtic Origins: New ways forward in archaeology, linguistics, and genetics*. Oxford: Oxbow

Ellis, P.B. 2008. *The Celts: A history*. Philadelphia, PA: Running Press

Evans, J., Fairholt, F.W. & Sellier, P. 1864. *The Coins of the Ancient Britons*. London: J. Russel Smith

Freedberg, D. 1991. *The Power of Images: Studies in the history and theory or response*. Chicago, IL: University of Chicago Press

Gell, A. 1998. *Art and Agency: An anthropological theory*. Oxford: Clarendon Press

Ghisleni, L. 2018. Contingent persistence: Continuity, change, and identity in the Romanization debate. *Current Anthropology* 59(2), 138–66

James, S. 1993. *Exploring the World of the Celts*. London: Thames and Hudson

James, S. 1999. *The Atlantic Celts: Ancient people or modern invention?* London: British Museum Press

Jenkins, S. 2022. *The Celts: A sceptical history*. London: Profile Books

de Jersey, P. 2001. *Celtic coinage in Britain*. Princes Risborough: Shire Archaeology 72

de Jersey, P. 2008. Evans and Ancient British coins. In A. MacGregor (ed.), *Sir John Evans 1823-1908*, pp 152–72. Oxford: Ashmolean Museum

Koch, J.T. & Carey, J. (2003) *The Celtic Heroic Age: Literary sources for ancient Celtic Europe & early Ireland & Wales*. 4th edn. Aberystwyth: Celtic Studies Publications

Kraay, C.M. & Hirmer, M. 1966. *Greek Coins*. London: Thames and Hudson

Leins, I. 2007. Coins in context: Coinage and votive deposition in Iron Age South East Leicestershire. *British Numismatics Journal* 77, 22–48

Leins, I. 2012. *Numismatic data reconsidered: Coin distributions and interpretation in studies of late Iron Age Britain*. Unpublsihed PhD Thesis, School of Historical Studies, Newcastle University

Leins, I. (ed.) 2015. *Celts: Art and Identity*. Exhibition catalogue. London: The British Museum Press

Lengyel, L. 1954. *L'art Gaulois dans les médailles*. Montrouge-Seine: Éditions Corvina

Lengyel, L. 1969. *Le secret des Celtes*. Les Hautes Plaines de Mane: R. Morel

Lilly, S. 2008. *Ancient Celtic Coin Art*. Glastonbury: Wooden

MacGregor, A. 2008. *Sir John Evans 1823-1908: Antiquity, commerce and natural science in the age of Darwin*. Oxford: Ashmolean Museum

Mack, R.P. 1964. *The Coinage of Ancient Britain*. 2nd edn. London: Spink

Megaw, R.M. & Megaw, J.V.S. 1986. *Early Celtic Art: In Britain and Ireland*. Princes Risborough: Shire Archaeology 38

Nash, D. 1987. *Coinage of the Celtic World*. London: Seaby

Nimura, C. 2015. *Prehistoric Rock Art in Scandinavia*. Oxford: Oxbow Books

Oppenheimer, S. 2007. *The Origins of the British*. London: Robinson

Mack, R.P. 1953. *The Coinage of Ancient Britain*. 1st edition. London: Spink & Son

Rich, M., Cottam, E. & Rudd, C. 2014. *Boar Horse*. Aylsham: Chris Rudd

Ross, A. 1967. *Pagan Celtic Britain: Studies in iconography and tradition*. London: Routledge and Kegan Paul

Rowlett, R.M. 1994. Did Iron Age Celts really hunt wild boar (Sus Scrofa)? *Proceedings of the Harvard Celtic Colloquium* 14, 195–210

Rudd, C. 2019. Hidden faces on Celtic coins. *Coin News* 2019 (Nov), 41–3

Rybot, N., Cottam, E. & Rudd, C. 2018. *War Coins of the Sun Warriors: Silver staters of the Coriosolites of Armorica, 56 BC*. Aylsham: Chris Rudd

Salway, P. 1993. *The Oxford Illustrated History of Roman Britain*. Oxford: Oxford University Press

Seaford, R. 2004. *Money and the Early Greek Mind*. Cambridge: Cambridge University Press

Sellwood, L. & Metcalf, D.M. 1986. A Celtic silver coin of previously unpublished type from St. Nicholas at Wade, Thanet: The prototype for Anglo-Saxon Sceattas 'BMC' Type 37? *The British Numismatic Journal* 56, 181–82

Shakespeare, W. & Pitcher, J. 2005. *Cymbeline*. London: Penguin

Sills, J. 2017. *Divided Kingdoms: The Iron Age gold coinage of Southern England*. Aylsham, Norfolk

Talbot, J.A. 2017. *Made for Trade: A new view of Icenian coinage*. Oxford: Oxbow Books

Thomson, H. 2013. *The Green Road into the Trees: A walk through England*. London: Windmill Books

Thorpe, L. & Geoffrey of Monmouth. 1966. *The History of the Kings of Britain*. Harmondsworth: Penguin

Van Arsdell, R.D. 1988. Celtic chicanery. *Spinks Numismatic Circular* 1988(96), 78

Van Arsdell, R.D. 1989. *Celtic Coinage of Britain*. London: Spink

Wells, P.S. 2012. *How Ancient Europeans Saw the World: Vision, patterns, and the shaping of the mind in prehistoric times*. Princeton, NJ: Princeton University Press

Woolf, G. 2014. Romanization 2.0 and its alternatives. *Archaeological Dialogues* 21, 45–50

Zanker, P. & Shapiro, H.A. 1988. *The Power of Images in the Age of Augustus*. Ann Arbor, MI: University of Michigan Press

Online Resources

Celtic Coins Index Digital: cci.arch.ox.ac.uk

Iron Age Coins in Britain: iacb.arch.ox.ac.uk

Classical Sources

Augustus. *Res Gestae Divi Augusti*. Translated by F. W. Shipley. Harvard University Press. 1924

Caesar. *The Gallic War*. Translated by H. J. Edwards. Harvard University Press. 1917

Dio Cassius. *Roman History VIII: Books 61-70*. Translated by E. Cary. Harvard University Press. 1925

Diodorus Siculus. *Library of History: Books 2.35-8*. Translated by C.H. Oldfather. Harvard University Press. 1935 and 1939

Herodotus. *The Histories*. Translated by A. de Sélincourt. Penguin. 1954

Pliny the Elder. *Natural History: A Selection*. Translated by J.F. Healy. Penguin. 2004

Strabo. *Geography: Books 3-5*. Translated by H.L. Jones. Harvard University Press. 1923

Suetonius. *Lives of the Caesars: Volume 1*. Translated by J.C. Rolfe. Harvard University Press. 1913 (revised 1998)

Tacitus. *Agricola*. Translated by M. Hutton and revised by R.M. Ogilvie. Harvard University Press. 1970

Tacitus. *Histories: I-V; Annals I-III*. Translated by C.H. Moore and J. Jackson. Harvard University Press. 1931

Tacitus. *Annals*. Translated by C. Damon. Penguin. 2012

INDEX